# Kenneth

by
Susan Lentz

Bloomington, IN  Milton Keynes, UK

*AuthorHouse™*
*1663 Liberty Drive, Suite 200*
*Bloomington, IN 47403*
*www.authorhouse.com*
*Phone: 1-800-839-8640*

*AuthorHouse™ UK Ltd.*
*500 Avebury Boulevard*
*Central Milton Keynes, MK9 2BE*
*www.authorhouse.co.uk*
*Phone: 08001974150*

*This book is a work of non-fiction. Unless otherwise noted, the author and the publisher make no explicit guarantees as to the accuracy of the information contained in this book and in some cases, names of people and places have been altered to protect their privacy.*

*First published by AuthorHouse 1/8/2007*

*ISBN: 978-1-4259-3960-1 (sc)*
*ISBN: 978-1-4259-3959-5 (hc)*

*Library of Congress Control Number: 2006904638*

*Printed in the United States of America*
*Bloomington, Indiana*

*This book is printed on acid-free paper.*

*Cover photograph by Richard Benson*
*Cover design by Amy Carner Hill*

To
Smith, Anna, Reynolds, John, Davidson,
Meredith, and Alison
- so that they may always remember their grandmother

# Contents

# Introduction

My mother loved Kenneth McDougall for sixty-one years. For almost seven of those years, he was alive.

They made a striking couple – he, tall and handsome; she, petite and beautiful with her big dimpled smile and dreamy, gentle nature.

World War II interrupted their life together. Kenneth joined the famed 10th Mountain Infantry Division and then moved on to fight in Italy and France with the First Special Service Force. Mother volunteered for the Army Nurse Corps and served in England with the 141st General Hospital unit.

When the war ended, Kenneth lived only in Mother's heart. But there he was very much alive, something my father accepted and my sisters and I never thought to question.

Elizabeth Barrett Browning's Sonnet XLIII from her <u>Sonnets from the Portuguese</u> provided the outline for this book. In a condolence letter, Mother's friend Louisa Rhine wrote that when she thought of how Mother must be suffering over the loss of her beloved Kenneth, she couldn't help but think of the last line of this poem, "…and, if God choose, I shall but love thee better after death."

Pearl Yarbrough

Kenneth McDougall

# Prologue

My mother was a fearless, intrepid traveler.  In the years just after World War II, a time when few women dared travel without a man, she loaded three children into an old car, tossed our battered suitcases in the trunk, and set off on a seven-hundred-mile drive without so much as a second thought.  She had been in the war, after all, and wasn't likely to be frightened of a car trip.

Since our father didn't like to travel, vacations were female affairs. Just Mother, my sisters Jane and Anne, and I made the long drive from Mississippi to North Carolina to see Mother's family, the Yarbroughs. We made this trip every summer when we were very young, then every year or so as we grew older.

The morning we left on vacation, Mother got up hours before dawn and slipped on a dress, nylon stockings, and a pair of low heels.  She pulled her straight brown hair up into a smooth French twist and then polished her look by adding a pair of earrings and her favorite necklace, a thick gold choker.  She patted a bit of powder across her cheeks and smoothed on a touch of deep red lipstick, the only makeup she ever wore.  Once dressed and ready, she kissed my father goodbye, settled my sisters and me in the backseat of her Chevrolet, and drove off into the darkness as though she were going to a luncheon rather than beginning a sixteen-hour drive.

We left home while it was still dark because it was cooler then and the car had no air conditioning.  Once the sun came up there was no respite from the heat.

The roads were too bumpy for reading, and my sisters and I soon tired of singing the same few songs.  We busied ourselves tallying the number of spotted cows we spied or copying down the license plate numbers of passing cars. Since Mother seldom drove over 45 miles an hour, she never actually passed anything other than cars parked on the side of the road. We jotted down those numbers, too. In our narrow 1950s world, seeing license plates from faraway states was exciting. It was almost like going there.

When boredom got the better of us and we began to fuss and fight, Mother distracted us with tales about the aunts, uncles, and cousins we were going to see in Winston-Salem. We had fourteen aunts and uncles and seventeen cousins awaiting our arrival, so there were a lot of stories to tell.

Sooner or later, we would tire of hearing about our family. Then Mother would tell us about the fun she and her friends had in nursing school or the interesting things she did in England during World War II. But our favorite stories were about the man she had once been engaged to, Kenneth. My sisters and I were infatuated with Kenneth and knew all the stories about him by heart. Even so, we never tired of hearing them. We especially loved the story of how they met: Mother had been living in Durham, North Carolina, at the time, doing private duty nursing. She was hired to care for the noted psychologist Dr. William McDougall, who was dying of cancer. When the doctor's son Kenneth came home from Scotland to help care for his father, Mother took one look at the handsome young veterinarian and fell madly in love.

Mother could keep us entranced for hours with her storytelling – a good thing since the drive took us two full days. We traveled via dusty back roads, dangerous two-lane highways, and terrifying mountain passes. I don't know how Mother stood it, except that it was the only way she could get to North Carolina.

As difficult as the long trip must have been for her, when we left Winston-Salem she often drove another eighty miles east, taking us on to Durham to see Mum and Angus McDougall. If any of our relatives thought it strange that we cut our visit short just to make this extra excursion, no one ever said anything. Our father certainly didn't begrudge us these visits. That was remarkably generous of him because Mum was the mother of Kenneth, the great love of my mother's life, and Angus was Kenneth's brother.

# I.
## *How do I love thee?*

Kenneth had lived at 408 Swift Avenue in Durham, although the word "avenue" is somewhat misleading. It more closely resembled a lane than a street back then, and was not nearly so grand as the word avenue implied. Very near the campus of Duke University, it was a quiet street in a friendly, close-knit neighborhood.

The McDougalls loved living there. They always referred to their modest home as "408" or "408 Swift Avenue" as though the address was the home's name. No one ever referred to it as "home" or "the house."

My sisters and I knew that 408 was a very special place, but we had no concept of the depth of emotion our mother must have felt when she pulled into that driveway. How many memories that house held for her! She and Kenneth, or Ken as she called him, began their romance there. It was where they planned to start their married life.

Mother had lived at 408 Swift Avenue, too. She moved in with Mum when Ken left for the Army in June of 1942 and stayed there – in Ken's room – until the end of 1943. After the war, she returned to Durham and once again moved into his room at 408. On our vacations, she stayed in this same room with all of his things and all of her memories.

Progress caught up with Swift Avenue around 1960 when the city widened the street, making it into a thoroughfare. In the process, Mum lost eight feet of her beloved front yard and the house seemed to move forward, no longer so well situated on its beautiful lot.

But at the time of our visits, 408 seemed to me a huge house set far back off its narrow ribbon of a street. Although it appeared to have two stories, the upstairs was really just an attic converted into a couple of bedrooms. Two-story houses signified great wealth to me back then, but in reality 408 Swift Avenue was only a small and tasteful cottage, a dollhouse really.

Inside and out, 408 was tidy and well cared for. To the left of the front door, ivy blanketed the white clapboard siding. A large wooden swing hung from the porch that ran along the right side of the house, hidden behind a lattice wall ablaze with red roses. Leafy green vines with brightly colored blossoms climbed the sides of the latticework, cooling and darkening the porch with a fragrant covering.

Inside, the home was quiet and filled with books – in bookcases, on shelves, and stacked on tabletops. The living room furniture was well-worn and comfortable, positioned around a fireplace that had seen considerable use. Most of the downstairs walls were covered in pine paneling softly darkened by age and the smoke of countless fires.

It was a cozy home, a place that seemed to imbue feelings of peace and contentment. One of the nicest things about it was Mum's parakeet Sweetie. I had never known anyone with such an exotic pet, living as I did in a world where people kept only dogs and cats. I fell in love with the little budgie and begged for a parakeet of my own, one to live in our kitchen just as Sweetie lived in Mum's. Mother, who probably didn't want anything more to care for, told me that parakeets were usually something only the English kept as pets. I was well aware that the McDougalls were an English family and that we were not. I accepted her explanation without question.

The McDougalls had immigrated to the United States in 1920, shortly before Ken's twelfth birthday. His father had resigned his position at Oxford University that year and joined the faculty at Harvard University.

After six years at Harvard, Dr. McDougall left Massachusetts and took his family on a year-long trip around the world. Upon returning to the States, the McDougalls moved to Durham where Ken's father established and chaired the psychology department at Duke University. Mum never moved again, and Angus, who lived elsewhere as a young man, eventually returned to settle down with his mother.

My sisters and I loved visiting Mum and Angus. We especially loved afternoons at 408 Swift Avenue where everyone observed the English custom of taking tea. Mother had prepared us well in advance, educating us at tea parties where she served real tea and talked about her favorite foods. She loved the shortbread, scones, and cucumber sandwiches she remembered from her days in England. My sisters and I drank up her instruction as happily as we would later drink the tea at Mum's.

Mum took her tea with milk, so all of us did the same. The idea of mixing milk with tea seemed strange to three little Southern girls, as strange as drinking tea without ice. Even Mother, the diehard black coffee drinker, enjoyed her milky tea almost as much as she enjoyed the refinement and civility of the ceremony. This was Mother at her happiest, a glimpse of life as she had thought it would be.

Mum serving tea in the living room at 408 Swift Avenue, 1953.

As different as everything seemed at the McDougalls', it felt comforting to be with Ken's family in a home that still resonated with so many memories of him. Being there ensconced among his things never seemed strange or awkward to us. We were always around Ken's things.

Jane, Anne, and I spent countless rainy days rummaging through the wooden box that contained Mother's vast collection of gifts and mementos from her years with Ken. Sometimes we snooped behind her back, but often she would sit down and sort through the box with us, telling us stories about the war, her life in England, and Ken.

Opening Mother's memory box transported us to an exciting, unfamiliar world. She had money from Algeria, Japan, and countries all over Europe: England, France, Germany, the Netherlands. The box overflowed with jewelry, multicolored ribbons and badges from World War II, cards, and letters – stacks of letters tied with blue satin ribbons. There were pictures of Mother when she was young and pictures of Ken, lots of pictures of Ken. We tried on jewelry he had given her, sorted through his letters and mementos, and admired the many photographs of him.

When we listened to Mother's stories about Ken, we couldn't help but wonder what our lives would be like if he had been our father. We chose to overlook the fact that, genetically speaking, we wouldn't exist. My sisters and I identified so closely with our mother that we felt certain we would have been born anyway. We conceded that we might look a bit different, but we never doubted that we would still be her daughters. In fact, we speculated that we might be an even better version of ourselves since the Ken that Mother described seemed to have no faults.

Of all the McDougalls, I felt that I knew Ken best. This man my mother loved so much seemed incredibly interesting. A veterinarian, he went on to earn a Ph. D. in zoology from Duke. He loved to camp and hike and appeared to know everything there was to know about plants, animals, insects, and reptiles. A fount of information on astronomy as well as the sea, Ken loved to swim, sail, and climb mountains. One of the world's leading authorities on gray seals and sea birds, he could identify most any bird by sight or song. He loved to garden and wrote beautiful love letters and poetry. A brilliant man with a wry sense of humor, Ken seemed both approachable and mythical, a handsome, pipe-smoking Englishman frozen in time at the prime of life. My sisters and I were enchanted with him.

We adored Ken's older brother, too. A tall man with patrician looks and a hint of red in his sandy brown hair, Angus personified the McDougalls' proud Scottish heritage. His looks could not have been more befitting his name had he walked around in a kilt – something he actually did on holidays and special occasions.

Angus was charming and cheerful, with courtly manners and an elegant style. A talented artist, he was the sculptor of Steuben's Glass Apple. He painted as well, and his oil of a small seaside cottage hung in our home as we were growing up.

Ken also had an older sister, Lesley, but I never knew her. She and Mother were great friends and corresponded for years, but Lesley lived far away so they seldom saw one another.

Angus, Mum, and Lesley on the front steps at 408 Swift Avenue.

I did know Ken's mother though, and remember her as being small, sweet, and very English. But what I remember most about Mum is how much my mother loved her. Mother cared so deeply about Mum that she gave my younger sister her name – Anne.

Mother and Mum maintained a close relationship for twenty-six years, visiting whenever Mother could get to Durham, exchanging long letters when she could not. They shared a terrible bond, both having loved Ken so much, but I don't remember our visits as being sad in any way. In fact, I remember them as being just the opposite.

My sisters and I loved to lie in Ken's attic bedroom at night, letting our eyes trace the many slopes and angles of the ceiling as it followed along the sharp roofline. We plied Mother with questions as she put us to bed, pointing at various things and asking if they had belonged to Ken, begging to examine anything he might have touched. She answered patiently as she tucked us in, her soft voice becoming even gentler as she spoke of him, a distant, faraway look in her eyes. Eventually she would put an end to our questions, smooth the bedcovers, kiss us goodnight, and go downstairs to spend time with Ken's mother.

Mother not only loved Mum, she also admired her courage and resilience. Years before Ken's death, Mum had lost her oldest son, Duncan, in a plane crash. A stunt pilot in Britain's Royal Air Force, Duncan lost his life in an air show. Mum had suffered the loss of her youngest child as well. Janet died of tuberculosis when she was only five or six years old.

Everyone who knew Anne McDougall felt that she was an extraordinarily strong woman, the heart and soul of a remarkable family – just the sort of family that Mother and Ken hoped to have.

# II.
## *Let me count the ways.*

In the fall of 1930, just as Mother moved from Winston-Salem to Durham to enter nursing school at Duke University, Ken left the city for Scotland to pursue a degree in veterinary medicine.

He graduated from the University of Edinburgh at the height of the Depression, a time when there were virtually no veterinary positions available. Ken chose to stay in his beloved Scotland anyway and spent the next few years doing research with the noted naturalist Dr. Frank Fraser Darling. Had Ken's family not been so far away, he might have stayed in Scotland forever.

But late in 1937, doctors at Duke Hospital found that William McDougall had incurable cancer. As soon as he got the news, Ken purchased a one-way ticket to the United States on the USS *City of Baltimore*. Dr. McDougall would soon need round-the-clock care, and Ken felt that his medical background could be helpful. When there was no nurse on duty, Ken administered his father's medications. When there was a nurse on duty, that nurse was Mother. Together, the two of them cared for Dr. McDougall during the final months of his life. Their working relationship quickly blossomed into romance.

On November 28, 1938, nearly a year after Mother began caring for him, Dr. McDougall died. With neither Angus nor Lesley living nearby, Ken was unwilling to leave his newly widowed mother alone. He enrolled in graduate school at Duke and began working toward a doctorate in zoology. Although Mother moved on to other employment, she and Ken continued to see one another.

Ken, taken in the Treshnish Isles off Scotland around 1936. He lived in these remote islands while doing research on sea birds and gray seals with Dr. Frank Fraser Darling.

About a year and a half into their courtship – on September 1, 1939 – an event occurred that altered Ken and Mother's lives forever. The conflict that had been brewing in Europe finally came to a head, a day the two of them referred to as "the day the bottom dropped out of the world." Germany invaded Poland.

Britain and France had a treaty with Poland, and on September 3 they declared war on Germany. Because Ken was a British citizen, a reporter interviewed him for a short article in the local paper. Ken told the reporter that he thought Britain had no choice but to go to war. He also said that he didn't think they would gain enough out of the conflict to justify the cost. This was a common assumption before the magnitude of the situation abroad unfolded.

Most Americans viewed the menacing acts that led up to World War II, especially the events prior to September 1, 1939, as "the trouble in Europe." It was a distant problem if a nagging one, but certainly nothing monumental enough to warrant intervention. Focused on recovering from the Great Depression, few Americans paid heed to the situation in Europe or the carnage taking place in Japanese-occupied China and Southeast Asia. The United States held fast to its isolationist policy.

Because such a large part of the population failed to grasp the gravity of the global situation, life in the U.S. went on as usual for most people. But not for Ken. He felt a strong sense of duty to his country and immediately began a letter-writing campaign to enlist in either the British or Canadian armed forces.

Mother wasn't enthusiastic about Ken joining the service. Nearly a year earlier, just after Dr. McDougall's death, she had had a disturbing dream about Ken's being in the military. Although she never thought of herself as psychic or prescient, Mother occasionally had extraordinarily prophetic dreams. This particular dream had bothered her so much that she had asked Ken to apply for American citizenship. Realizing that England might eventually become involved in the European conflict, Mother had felt confident that the U.S. wouldn't. She thought that if Ken were American, he would be safely out of harm's way when trouble started.

Ken had seen the situation differently and had told Mother that he didn't feel he should be naturalized then, saying, "If war comes, it comes, and nationality won't make much difference in the end. Everything must come to an end sometime. One can do worse than die fighting for his country, be the cause good or bad. One man has no meaning at all on the face of the earth."

Joining the military proved more difficult than Ken had anticipated. Early in the war, Britain had no firm policy on what to do about foreign nationals. Officials replied to Ken's inquiries by telling him they couldn't assure him that he would be accepted even if he returned to England to enlist. The military wanted men with mechanical or technical skills, citing a more immediate need for machinery than men. Ken persisted, writing letters to various personnel at both the British Embassy and Consulate. Officials politely rebuffed his offers by referring him to yet another attaché or secretary.

Canadian officials acknowledged his letters by writing that Ken's educational background would necessitate his becoming an officer and that they were only commissioning men already in the military. He continued his inquiries to the Canadians, but ran into a formidable obstacle: In order to enlist, he had to present himself in person. Ken had entered the United States under the British quota, allowing him to live and work in America for an extended period of time. Leaving the U.S. meant losing that status. If the Canadian Army interviewed Ken and then rejected him, he wouldn't be allowed to return to Durham as anything more than a visitor.

Ken applied for a re-entry permit from American authorities and approached the Canadian Air Force. The CAF replied that their quota for trainees had been filled and they could only add his name to a waiting list.

Returning to England to enlist was a difficult, unsettling proposition. Ken had no job awaiting him there, no means of support in the event the military didn't accept him. With travel abroad stymied by a lack of passenger service and the danger posed by German submarines patrolling the Atlantic, Ken had few options.

Because he could do little else, he continued his studies, persistently writing officials here, in England, and in Canada. All of those he wrote let him know that they appreciated his desire to serve, but none encouraged him. Their lack of interest gave him time to establish a deeper relationship with Mother.

When they met in 1938, Mother was twenty-six, Ken twenty-nine. At first glance, they must have appeared an unlikely pair. Ken, a reserved and brilliant man, sometimes referred to himself as being a bit of a "dour Scot." He enjoyed solitary activities and felt that he was a poor mixer socially. Talkative, outgoing Mother never missed a party or met a stranger. Blessed with a sunny disposition, she saw the good in every situation. She believed that people were as happy as they wanted to be, and she wanted to be happy.

More precisely, she wanted to be happy with Ken. The two of them enjoyed simple pleasures like movies, picnics, and long walks in the countryside. Strolling the banks of the Eno River was a popular pastime in those days. Ken and Mother spent many evenings sitting on an old bench overlooking the river, admiring the moon and its reflection shimmering in the water. Later, from opposite sides of the country and then opposite sides of the world, they wrote about looking up at the moon and remembering those happy times.

Although both Ken and Mother lived in Durham, work occasionally separated them. Ken spent summers doing research at Duke's Marine Laboratory in Beaufort, North Carolina. Mother did a lot of newborn nursing, accompanying a new baby home from the hospital and caring for it while the mother recovered. Nurses stayed with their new charges for a month or more, and sometimes the families lived out of town. Long distance phone calls were expensive in those days; most people relied on the postal service to stay in touch.

Ken and Mother corresponded frequently. Their letters were always eloquent and beautifully composed, if somewhat formal at first. Over time the letters evolved into a more intimate, conversational style full of their feelings for each other and reminiscences about their good times together. By the summer of 1940, however, the tone of Ken's letters began to change markedly. Although they seem to be written by a more serious suitor, an unmistakable air of depression hung over his words.

Ken's efforts to join the military were continuing to prove fruitless and frustrating. Almost a year into the war, his friends and relatives in England faced countless hardships. Ken felt guilty about his own easy life and embarrassed to be studying in America at such a time.

Overseas, things were not going well. Germany had overrun most of Western Europe. When France fell in June of 1940, the British found themselves alone, the Isles effectively surrounded by German-held land on the continent. Russia, a marginal ally at best, still honored its shameful nonaggression pact with the Nazis, and the majority of Americans continued to oppose any involvement in a foreign war.

Once France fell, Germany felt in a position to conquer Britain and end the war victoriously. When the British refused his terms of surrender, an enraged Hitler threatened invasion. He ordered his Luftwaffe to destroy the Royal Air Force, Britain's formidable defense system. In July, German air forces launched the series of attacks that began The Battle of Britain, a fight for the skies over the British Isles.

The Royal Air Force rose to the challenge, extracting heavy losses from the much larger Luftwaffe. By September, Germany had been forced to change aerial tactics several times, finally resorting to bombing British cities in an effort to undermine national resolve.

Along with the RAF, British ground forces put up a heroic defense, and by the end of October the Battle of Britain was effectively over. Unwilling to send troops ashore while the Royal Air Force still dominated the skies, a frustrated Germany postponed its planned invasion. As 1940 ended, Hitler turned his attention to the east and began making plans to invade Russia.

By January 1941, Ken and Mother had known each other for three years. She was ready for their relationship to evolve into marriage. With the world situation so tenuous, Ken felt that his future was too uncertain to make a lifelong commitment, for her sake as much as his own. Although he saw war as "the most ridiculous of all human activities," he had no intention of sitting out the conflict. He continued his letter-writing campaign to find a place in the armed forces, but Britain, faced with the new realities of an air war, needed pilots and mechanics. Thirty-two years old, with no flying experience or mechanical skills, Ken wasn't a likely candidate. His letters went unanswered.

On December 7, 1941, Japan attacked Pearl Harbor and American men began enlisting in droves. Ken turned his attention to joining the U.S. military, but there was a question as to eligibility since he wasn't a citizen. The Navy did not accept aliens as volunteers. Although everyone seemed to agree that the Army did, no one in authority could tell Ken exactly how to proceed. He began the process of naturalization hoping to obtain a draft number.

As Ken finalized his plans, Mother wrestled with difficult decisions of her own. The military encouraged nurses to enlist, but Ken, concerned that she felt pressured to join, tried to dissuade her. He attempted to steer her toward various government jobs that would assuage her conscience yet spare her the danger and uncertainty of life in the armed forces. He felt that she was doing essential work already and shouldn't put herself in jeopardy. But Mother longed to do something meaningful, a job directly related to the war effort. She wanted to go where she was really needed and endlessly debated how she might be most useful.

Ken finally managed to enlist in the U.S. Army in spite of his alien status. His inability to join the war any earlier had given him and Mother the gift of almost three years together in Durham and allowed him to finish his Ph. D. in zoology. He graduated from Duke University on May 23, 1942, and by June 10, he was at Fort Bragg, North Carolina. Thirty-three years old, Ken was almost ten years older than the average recruit. But for him, being there was a matter of conscience.

# III.

*I love thee to the depth and breadth and height*
*My soul can reach,*

Ken had grown up leading a rather cosseted life. His father had been on the faculty of one prestigious university after another, and Ken had spent more than half his life in England with its firmly entrenched class system. But in the summer of 1942, he found himself at Fort Bragg meeting – and enjoying – a melting pot of humanity. In a postcard dated June 19, he told Mother that he had "spent a jolly day slinging garbage with a 6'4" athletic instructor from Boone and a 5'2" ex-concrete mixer who poured all the concrete for Duke Stadium. What a world! What an army!"

Admitting that being in the military wasn't as bad as he had expected, Ken found that he rather liked being on an equal footing with the other recruits, saying they were a "pleasant, friendly lot…This life is going to suit me all right."

Fort Bragg was a bustling place in the early months of the war, with everybody constantly on the move. There wasn't much respect for Ph.D.s though; Ken's jobs included picking up cigarette butts and cleaning latrines. He seemed to do an inordinate amount of digging, which he laughed off, writing, "You see that my long suppressed penchant for ditch digging is at last being gratified."

One hot, sticky Sunday that June, Mother and Mum drove down to Fort Bragg to see Ken. Squinting in the bright sunlight of a sweltering summer day, he and Mother had their picture taken standing in front of a big, black car. He is tall and thin and looks more like a Boy Scout than a soldier in his rumpled uniform. Mother stands alongside him, smiling gamely in her pretty flowered dress.

Ken and Mother, Fort Bragg, North Carolina, June 1942.

Ken sent Mother the picture a few weeks later, commenting that the photo hadn't turned out very well and that they would do better the next time. He worried that she had come away with "an awful impression of Fort Bragg, what with the heat and the flies." But, it's a good thing that Mother found the time and the gasoline to drive down that Sunday. The next morning Ken received orders to report to Fort Lewis, Washington.

It was at Fort Lewis that Ken's training began in earnest. Soon after arriving, he wrote Mother a long, enthusiastic letter describing his new life. He told her how beautifully situated the fort was and said that he was learning the parts of a rifle, how to pitch a shelter tent, and all sorts of "marching steps."

Although he had no trouble with the weapons or the more physically strenuous activities, Duke's Phi Beta Kappa graduate had a hard time with those marching steps, saying, "My particular difficulty is in understanding the commands, with the result that the squad and I sometimes march off in opposite directions, or collide head on. It is somewhat embarrassing. However, Corporal Goodman is a good egg, and takes it with a suppressed grin.

"I also find great difficulty in taking 30 inch steps without falling down all the time. Oh well, I can keep up with the book work at least." Eventually Ken managed to master the marching and soon qualified as "expert" in small-bore rifle fire.

Ken's letters from Fort Lewis mention the large number of accomplished skiers and mountaineers in his outfit and the exciting prospect of skiing and climbing exercises in the nearby mountains. He could barely contain his excitement as he described their large mule train, but that novelty wore off quickly. He came to hate those "vicious, smelly beasts" and managed to keep his veterinary past a closely guarded secret.

In a pattern of behavior evident throughout the war, Ken made the best of his situation. Not one to waste time complaining, he kept busy, taking advantage of every available sightseeing opportunity. Located about ten miles south of Tacoma, Washington, Fort Lewis was a 62,000-acre military reservation in 1942.

Mother had never been to the Pacific Northwest, so Ken wrote her long letters with detailed descriptions of the spruce and hemlock forests he saw on his hikes. He raved about Washington's beautiful, snow-capped mountains and the incredible views of Puget Sound.

One day, engrossed in exploring his new territory, Ken inadvertently wandered off the massive base. When he started back to barracks and a Military Policeman stopped him asking to see a pass, Ken realized that he had somehow gone AWOL. A few tense moments ensued, but he found that the MP was not only a good fellow, but a busy one as well. Ken quietly slipped back to his barracks home.

Relieved to have avoided trouble, he questioned why an infantryman – of all people – wasn't allowed to walk around as much as he might want. That made little sense to Ken's wandering spirit, but his desire to hike during his free time made no sense at all to other men in the company.

In their off hours, most of the younger men raced into town to bars and dances, activities Ken had no interest in pursuing. If not exploring, he was looking for a quiet place to read. A voracious reader, he constantly ordered books and asked Mum to send along books she had finished. As much as he enjoyed the company of other men, Ken liked quiet time alone. He found that commodity in short supply in the Army.

Soldiers at Fort Lewis had no way of knowing that they were part of something that would prove to be historic. They had joined the new 87th Mountain Infantry Regiment which, along with later-formed regiments, became the famed 10th Mountain Infantry Division.

The 87th was the only unit in the Army recruited by a civilian, Charles Minot (Minnie) Dole, creator of the National Ski Patrol. Formed to provide the Army with an outfit capable of routing Germany's crack mountain troops, recruiters visited the ski teams of universities as well as ski schools across the country. There was competition to join the elite group, and applicants had to present letters of recommendation.

After the initial run on ski schools and universities, Dole began to round out the ranks, bringing in men with a variety of mountain experience – climbers, foresters, alpine guides, lumberjacks, and the like. Although Ken didn't know how to ski, he had hiked the Appalachian Trail, climbed in the Swiss Alps, and tackled some of the roughest country in England and Scotland. He had read about the new mountain troops forming out west and showed up at Fort Bragg with letters recommending him for Dole's unit.

Ken climbing Gimmer Crag, Langdon Pikes,
in England's Lake District around 1935.

When Ken joined the 87th Regiment, it was a virtual roll call of America's top climbers and skiers, many of whom were immigrants from countries under German occupation. Most of these men moved on to train in Colorado, where many of them fell in love with the beauty of the Rocky Mountains. After the war, a number of men returned to their old training grounds to open the ski resort of Vail and to develop Aspen into a world-class destination. Others opened, constructed, or instructed in almost every ski resort in the country. The men of the 10th Mountain Division generally receive credit for starting the ski industry enjoyed in America today.

But in 1942, these were still adventurous young men learning new skills and perfecting old ones. Without realizing it, they were building relationships that would last a lifetime. Ken felt quite lucky to be among them, as he was the last man assigned to E Company, the regiment's basic training unit.

Ken found his fellow soldiers to be a friendly group, and he gave Mother a good sense of barracks life when he wrote that it was hard to concentrate on the letter he was writing because, "The radio is blaring out jazz, as always. Six or eight of the boys are practicing 'Inspection Arms' with a good deal of hilarity, and half a dozen others are yelling derisive remarks. Every now and then someone or other wanders through on his way upstairs and stops for a brief wrestling match.

"Henry Chase, our local rowdywag, is sitting on the next bed to mine guzzling a pint of ice cream and carrying on a glittering repartee with several people at once, among them Corporal Marek, a Czech with a face like old iron and the soul of a child. Elmer Griffin, a tall ex-telephone lineman with fallen arches, is telling lurid tales about a maniacal epileptic friend of his. And that only begins to list the multifarious activities going on all over the barracks – all over Fort Lewis for that matter."

Somewhat reclusive by nature, Ken admitted that all the camaraderie was a new experience for him. Being with the same men twenty-four hours a day, he found that he had a lot in common with his fellow soldiers and couldn't help but make friends. Life in the Army was very different from the quiet, intellectually-oriented life that Ken had always known, but he seemed to enjoy the chaos.

Ken turned down the offer of a cushy job in the 87th Regiment's supply organization. Although he wanted to advance himself, he intended to lead men in combat, not work in an office. E Company was just where Ken wanted to be, and he was willing to make sacrifices to stay there. Only a few weeks into his training, a letter to Mother showed the strong bond growing among the men.

"You are going to be disappointed in me. Last week we were given the opportunity to apply for officer's training, and I didn't sign up. Those who are accepted will be sent to Fort Benning, Georgia, for the 90-day course, from which they will emerge as 2nd Lt. The snag is that they are very unlikely to return to this same regiment afterwards, as the army considers it unwise. They will be assigned to some regular infantry unit, probably. I would rather be a private or a non-com in this outfit than a general in any other, so here I stay unless and until they promise me a safe return. There are plenty of others who feel the same way about it, so it is possible that some arrangement may be worked out later on."

As he settled into army life, Ken had only one real problem with his situation, and that was the fact that Mother was over 3,000 miles away. He missed her desperately and wrote that her "ears must often burn, especially between ten and ten-thirty pm western war time," when he lay in bed and thought of all their good times together.

Seven weeks after he arrived at Fort Lewis, Ken's commanding officer called him in and told him that the Army needed volunteers willing to live outdoors under harsh winter conditions to test the new mountaineering equipment. Asked if he would be interested in spending the next few months camped high in the Rocky Mountains, Ken jumped at the opportunity.

The men chosen for this new Mountain Test Detachment spent a busy day loading several mule teams and five truckloads of equipment on an eastbound freight train. The next day, an excited group of soldiers left Fort Lewis for Colorado.

On August 20, 1942, Ken stepped off the train in a depressed little village called Aspen.

# IV.

## *...when feeling out of sight*

The Mountain Test Detachment, or Aspen Detachment, consisted of sixty-four men chosen from companies throughout the 87th Regiment. Half the detachment was made up of climbers, the other half muleteers learning their trade under alpine conditions. A diverse lot, the men hailed from Austria, England, Finland, France, Switzerland, Scotland, the U.S., Denmark, and, incredibly, Germany and Italy. Their orders were to spend three months in the Rockies testing the Army's new winter clothing as well as the tools and equipment necessary to support mountain fighting.

Ken's new assignment got off to a rather inauspicious beginning. "We arrived on Thursday, after a very cramped three days in the train. Unfortunately, we got there before our supplies did, so we had to 'live off the country' for two days – It was pretty lean pickings too. The railway people kindly left us the two Pullman cars to sleep in (two men to each berth!) and the local hotel did its best to feed us."

Aspen's local hotel was the Hotel Jerome, future home-away-from-home to the men of the 10th Mountain Infantry Division. Built in 1889, during Aspen's flush days as a mining center, the grand old hotel represented civilization to the soldiers. A favorite of all the men in the detachment, Ken got to know the Jerome intimately.

"As there was nothing else to do, I volunteered for K.P. and got stuck with it for both days, and what days! We started in at 5:00 a.m. and finished after 10:00 p.m. The hotel kitchen was an enormous place, filled with an extraordinary variety of equipment. Every single thing was filthy dirty and had to be scrubbed and scoured. By the time we left, I'm sure it was cleaner than it had been in fifty years. The reward for our labors was an ice cream machine which disgorged vast quantities of ice cream at the turn of a lever – K.P.s you know, have certain privileges."

When the mules and supplies finally arrived, men pitched camp along the edge of a forest in a valley about thirteen miles from Aspen. They chose as their site the upper border of a wide mountain meadow that sloped down towards a stream. Behind the campsite, dense forests of aspen poplars covered the hillsides.

Before pitching the fifteen large tents, men had to build a level foundation on which to set them. Ken helped build the stone retaining walls necessary to brace the foundation, a skill he had learned in Scotland years earlier. "Another of those apparently useless accomplishments turned to good account."

Camp life was primitive. The washroom was nothing more than a wooden rack lined with tin basins holding water dipped from a creek. At first men bathed in a large stream, but by late summer its water temperature had cooled to near freezing. Even the hardiest soldiers soon gave up on the idea of a bath in running water.

Everyone ate outside unless foul weather drove them into their tents, but the views made up for any discomfort. "When the cook yells 'CHOW!' we stream up the hill with our mugs and billycans. Hot food is ladled out of steaming cauldrons as we file past. Then we sit and eat under the trees, looking out to the wooded slopes of a great mountain across the valley.

"Upstream the valley opens up a little and gives us tantalizing glimpses of several fourteen thousand footers. Above the timberline huge buttresses and jagged ridges of gray rock lead up to snowy summits."

In time the men built a wooden mess hall. While laying its stone fireplace, they set into the mantle a wine bottle inscribed with the name of every man in the detachment. Divided according to rank, the roll lists names alphabetically under each heading. There are sixty-four names on the bottle, printed in tiny, precise black letters set on a white background. "Kenneth McDougall" is among twenty-three privates, surrounded by names familiar from his letters home.

Wine bottle listing the names of men in the Aspen Detachment.
*Photo from the collection of Ralph Lafferty.*

Inside the five-man tents, efficient little wood stoves and down-filled sleeping bags kept the soldiers comfortable. Ken and his tentmates managed to procure a Coleman gasoline lamp, making tent number 5 a popular place to gather in the evenings, as other men had only candles to provide light. "By ones and twos visitors from other tents creep in under the flap, and by eight o'clock we have a full house and pandemonium reigns until bedtime. At the moment there are ten people in our tent, all doing different things and carrying on five or six exceedingly loud and mostly highly obscene conversations.

"Jack Benson, who is washing his feet, is responsible for the blotches at the top of this page. Wilson Ware is trying to shave and keeps getting tangled up in other peoples' feet and spilling his hot water out of the old tomato can. Corporal Lamb squats in the middle of the floor, like me, trying to write a letter, and getting sawdust in his shoes. Corp. Whittemore is going over some photographs with a running commentary. Leo Block, an Austrian, keeps interrupting Leny Woods' lewd stories with loud and irrelevant comments. Fritz Kramer and Ix Vorn are poring over month old magazines with appropriate comments – and so on and so on."

Each night someone had to forgo socializing to take a turn at guard duty. As difficult as he found it to stay awake after a long day's work, Ken craved the solitude that night watch provided. He enjoyed the quiet hours alone, his reverie broken only by an occasional walk around the mule corral to scare off rats and wild animals. He relished having time to sit and stoke the roaring campfire, time to read, whittle, or just poke idly at the burning wood, lost in thoughts of home.

Days were busier than nights in the mountains. Once the men set up their campsite, they tackled their first assignment – building a suspension bridge across a 175-foot gorge. Ken's favorite job was rigging, which involved hanging from a steel cable to attach crosspieces. They managed to do a credible job with the bridge and soon both men and mules were able to cross without incident.

Later, soldiers undertook the seemingly impossible task of building a 1,500-foot cableway. With little machinery available, the men tied a thin rope around the waist of the best climber, Floyd "Wind River Joe" Wilson, and sent him down one side of a steep canyon and up the other side. Using the rope to guide the initial cable across, they grounded the heavy wire on both sides of the ravine and built from there.

A picture shows Ken using the cable as a zip line – legs drawn up to his chest, pipe clamped between his teeth. Happy and relaxed, he dangles over a seemingly bottomless mountain gorge.

Ken on a zip line, September 10, 1942, Aspen, Colorado.

The men continued tackling and succeeding at other equally daunting tasks, although according to Ken they didn't understand the reasoning behind many of their assignments. They built a bridge, but it didn't lead anywhere. "Are we being taught by the engineers or are we showing them? Nobody seems to know or to care particularly."

Once established on the mountainside, soldiers invited the local Aspenites up to look things over. Ken described the townspeople as a "wild and wooly lot," and almost all of them turned out for the big event. They rolled into camp aboard a variety of ancient vehicles and proceeded to swarm over the place, taking stock of everything and asking a multitude of questions about the men's tents, weapons, clothing, mules, and climbing equipment.

When the open house ended, a number of soldiers returned to Aspen with the locals for a night on the town. Referring to Aspen in his letters, Ken often put the word town in quotes. It was only a town by default really since there was little else around in such wild country. The mountains and countryside were unspoiled in 1942, inhabited by bears and deer, peopled by sheep ranchers and old miners.

Soldiers often climbed and hiked in the mountains, and occasionally they stumbled upon abandoned gold and silver mines. At one time Aspen had hosted a massive influx of prospectors, but after the mining boom waned, the area had become prime sheep raising country. Once, Ken ran into two shepherds mounted on horseback, their dogs herding the flock up a rugged mountainside. He stopped to speak with the men and learned that 10,000 sheep moved up the valley every spring, headed to high pastures for summer grazing.

Ken referred to their camp as being beautifully situated, but Aspen itself as "a very decrepit little place, formerly a prosperous mining center and now just managing to carry on as a skiing resort." Small and unrefined though it may have been, Aspen did have one major draw for Ken – the Hotel Jerome. With its steam heat, electric lights, and hot and cold running water, the Jerome was an oasis, a place to soak in a hot bath and sleep between real sheets. Ken walked to the hotel one afternoon in the early autumn of 1942, taking the twenty-five-mile scenic route into Aspen.

The first five miles of the way were on an old mining road leading to Taylor Pass on the Continental Divide. Initially the road wound through aspen woods where the "fallen leaves gleamed like golden guineas under foot." As he continued his climb, the aspens' pale green bark and delicate foliage gave way to a pine forest, its delicious smell magnified by the hot sunshine. Still higher, the pine trees became smaller and sparser.

Ken posed in uniform on a trail near Aspen.

Ken spied bare granite rock where small, colorful flowers managed to grow from within the tiniest cracks. There were magnificent views from the pass, and Taylor Lake reflected bright, white clouds scurrying across the sky.

Leaving the pass, Ken made his way down to an old drove road that ran for miles along a wide ridge, winding through forests of spruce and miles of open meadows. Porcupines waddled off into the woods on his approach, and coyotes howled as the sun went down behind the mountains. Long after dark, Ken ambled into Aspen and checked into the Jerome.

The next day, he hiked back to camp without benefit of roads, starting up a long wide valley with high, snowcapped summits on either side. On that fall day, aspen trees on the lower slopes flashed like orange and yellow flames between the tall green spires of spruce trees. Ken met fat woodchucks that stood on their hind legs and whistled at him. Garter snakes glided quietly into piles of dead sticks as he walked by, and the rattle of kingfishers echoed from mountain streams. He climbed out of the valley and a few hours later arrived on the crest of a ridge almost 14,000 feet high.

The mountains were sharp and clear in the autumn air. The first light snows had already settled on the jagged peaks, and Ken thought the resulting black and white contrast made the mountains look like steel engravings. The dusting of snow and strengthening winds signaled the coming of winter, a change Ken found invigorating. "The wind is like a huge, invisible and playful monster, so strong and determined that you are just a little afraid. Leaning into it, your coat snapping about your knees, you swallow huge gulps of cold air, and have trouble getting it out again. On such occasions a man feels a little more than human, as if the wind had infused him with some of its wild energy."

Rejuvenated, Ken headed down the mountain, working his way over to camp in the next valley. Along the way he indulged in one of his favorite pastimes, lying in a willow thicket to watch beavers at work on their dams. Entranced, he watched the little animals fell green aspen trees and store them beneath the water to provide food during the long mountain winter. The beavers were damming the waters deep, a sign that the coming winter would be especially cold. Water would need to be very deep not to freeze solid. Ken had been seeing the results of beaver activity near his work area and waiting impatiently for a chance to observe them up close.

A hot bath and a clean bed may have been the ostensible goals of his travel, but for Ken the real enjoyment lay in the trip itself. Passionate about hiking, Colorado's rugged mountains presented him with experiences very different from those he had enjoyed in North Carolina's soft, green, Smoky Mountains.

Ken had trekked through the Smokies numerous times, once hiking part of the new Appalachian Trail from Mt. Oglethorpe in Georgia to North Carolina. His postcard to Mother – written 154 miles into the trip – reported an encounter with a rattlesnake and a bear, but those dangers barely rated a mention. Instead, he waxed on about the beauty of the mountains and the exciting prospect of reaching the summit of the Smokies, Clingmans Dome.

The letters Ken wrote from Colorado included the same sort of information. He described the mountains he saw, their plants and animals. He marveled at the sight of jagged granite spires thrusting themselves into the brilliant Colorado sky. He wrote long letters detailing the way those same spires softened as they descended, eventually melting into sheer rock walls hundreds of feet tall. Barren at their heights, Ken explained that the walls slowly began to reveal signs of life as they distanced themselves from the icy wind at their summits. He told Mother how to spot the first hints of a tree line – growth so scraggly, bent, and dwarfed that it was barely recognizable. Ken noted how the trees struggled to hold on in their inhospitable environment, yet became progressively taller and thicker as they made their way down the mountainside and into more inviting territory. There, he observed, small stands of trees began to grow and multiply, eventually merging into lush green forests by the time they neared the valley floor.

Although Ken loved to venture out alone, he also liked to climb and hike with friends. He did a lot of exploring with his tentmate Dick Whittemore, a Harvard graduate from Connecticut, and Fred Craig, who Ken described as "a great hulk of a fellow, strong as a bull and twice as active, a true wanderer if ever there was one." But his usual companions were Wilson Ware and Red Kellar. The three of them spent almost all of their free time roaming the surrounding mountains, once covering forty-five miles in one twenty-hour day. They sometimes camped overnight, building a fire between two large stones to cook fish caught in nearby streams. After dinner, they piled spruce branches to make beds. Then, stretched out in their snug, down-filled sleeping bags, the men lay awake for hours watching the constellations wheel across the sky and planning "trips to the back of beyond for after the war."

Ralph Lafferty, second in command of the Aspen Detachment, and Dick Whittemore (on right) climbing Maroon Bells, 1942.
*Photo from the collection of Ralph Lafferty.*

Ken, Wilson, and Red made a diverse group: an English scientist, an aspiring playwright, and an ex-forester. Wilson, who reminded Ken of his brother Angus, was "a charming, lanky New Yorker" with a telltale accent, a former drama student at Yale. Red had "tried every type of job at one time or another and quit them all to climb." Red taught Ken and Wilson how to tell sheep tracks from deer tracks and whether the deer tracks were those of a doe or a buck.

Nothing – good or bad – seemed to last very long in the Army. After only three months, officers ordered the men to tear down everything they had built, pack up the valuable equipment, and move to a new camp about twelve miles north of Leadville, Colorado. There, at Camp

Hale, quite a surprise awaited them. They arrived on November 6 to a sea of mud, the caterwauling of machinery, and a vast number of construction workers milling about the unfinished camp, all doing "as little as possible."

The Aspen Detachment was the first of the line troops to arrive at Camp Hale, a massive camp in Pando, Colorado, that became the home of the 10th Mountain Division. Despite initial feelings of having barged in where they weren't wanted, things started out pleasantly enough. Ken began a series of intensive ski lessons, often requiring six hours a day on the slopes. There was only one other man in the beginner class, and they had the best instructor chosen from a group of world-class skiers.

Relieved that Mother wasn't there to witness his first attempts, Ken admitted, "I spent about 98 percent of my time climbing up the hill, and the other two percent coming down it in a quite astonishing series of gyrations."

When he wasn't learning to ski, Ken often served as "dog bait." In addition to messenger dogs, mountain troops used attack dogs. Ken's job was to hide high in the mountains so the animals could seek him out. When the dogs found him, trainers restrained them on strong leashes while Ken teased the animals and encouraged them to sink their teeth into the huge "false arm" he wore.

All too soon, a colonel arrived at Camp Hale. He canceled their pleasant occupations and ordered the soldiers to clean the new barracks and ready them for the troops that would soon arrive. Awakened at daybreak and sent out into the freezing cold with mops and brooms, men of the Aspen Detachment cleaned and swept all day. They stopped only to switch to shovels in an effort to stay ahead of the mud that covered everything. The only other possible assignment was kitchen duty, or KP, which was even worse than cleaning detail as those men spent sixteen-hour days in the mess hall. Ken wrote, "We are all in a state of rebellious depression, and wish ourselves back at Aspen."

As the population at Camp Hale grew, officers began breaking up the detachment, dispersing its members among several different companies. A close group, bonded by shared experiences, the men had hoped to stay together. When the Army canceled most of their promised leave time morale plummeted. Ken talked of moving to the newly forming 86th Regiment with Leonard Estrin, his former Top

Sergeant from Aspen. He also began to reconsider Officer Candidate School, as there was now the possibility he could return to the mountain troops.

The Army did not like to return newly commissioned officers to their former units. Officials felt that the relationship between new officers and their enlisted friends might be too close to ensure the degree of respect needed to command men in combat. Now that the 86th Regiment was forming, however, new officers had an option available. Assured they could rejoin the mountain troops, some men were willing to take on the responsibilities of leadership.

As 1942 ended, Ken and several close friends prepared to leave Colorado for Officer Candidate School. Shortly before their departure, the rest of the 87th Regiment arrived in camp. These old friends had stayed on at Fort Lewis when the detachment set out for Aspen in August. They had gone to Jolon, California, for their own training and maneuvers in the mountains, but once Camp Hale opened, the regiment reunited. There were almost five months of stories and escapades to catch up on, and as Ken said, they were still doing what they did best together: arguing.

# V.

*For the ends of Being and ideal Grace.*

In early January, 1943, Ken left Colorado for Fort Benning, Georgia. "Twenty of us left Camp Hale for O.C.S. last Sunday. We were the unhappy victims of bungling right up to the last moment. The parting touch was an eight-hour wait in the train station. We had a whole Pullman to ourselves in which we camped like a lot of gypsies. It must have been hitched to at least ten different trains in the course of the trip. About half the time, however, it was standing motionless in some siding or other. Whenever that happened we all boiled out and scoured the neighborhood for food and amusement. Upon Pueblo, Kansas City, St. Louis, Birmingham, and many lesser places, we descended like a swarm of locusts, seeking what we might devour. Everywhere the USO did a good job of entertaining us."

A member of class number 221, Ken described the course as incredibly difficult, citing the large number of men in each session that didn't make the grade and were sent back to the ranks. He worried that he might be among those weeded out as he had less military knowledge than most of his classmates. Ken had received only seven weeks of basic training before going to the decidedly unmilitary atmosphere he had enjoyed at Aspen. He tried to remain optimistic about his chances at O.C.S. though, saying, "Some awful fools seem to get through."

Ken felt that the instruction at Fort Benning was the best he ever had. Kept busy six days a week, he was still glad to be so near North Carolina. The first morning in Georgia, he had awakened to the familiar sight of pine trees growing out of red clay soil. He found being back in the South comforting after being away so long, saying, "Even the feel of the air against your skin and the shape and number of the clouds overhead are a relief from the hard brilliance of Colorado. I can't wait for it to rain. It will be the first I've seen in five months."

There was much to learn at Officer Candidate School, both from textbooks and constant field exercises. Fair weather or foul, mock battles went on all the time. Ken began to get an idea of how difficult it would be to control large numbers of men under the best of circumstances and wondered how one ever managed to do so in the heat of battle. He must have shown an aptitude for leadership though. On one exercise, when men had to pick a leader from each group, Ken's group chose him. Pleased, he wrote Mum that he "had been wondering whether these tough, carefree Americans would be willing to follow a doctor of philosophy with an English accent. Apparently they are."

At Fort Benning, rumors circulated about disarray in the mountain troops. Instructors encouraged candidates from the 10th Mountain Division to join the Rangers or one of the new paratrooper divisions. Although Ken had always wanted to try parachuting, if he couldn't return to Camp Hale he planned to join the Rangers. He thought his age might present a problem in either unit, saying, "Anyone over twenty-five is an old fogy around here."

At O.C.S., classes went on from early morning until late evening. Men got half an hour for meals and ten minutes free between classes. Ken used those short breaks to wolf down one of the five or more candy bars he consumed every day. His only time off was Sunday, and like all the other candidates, Ken spent that day studying and cleaning equipment. There was no leave time available until graduation day, April 19, 1943.

With ten days free, Ken couldn't get back to Durham fast enough! He spent the beautiful spring days with Mother, working side by side in the rose garden at 408.

He had a picture made during this trip home. On the back of the photograph Mum penned the words *Kenneth – 1943 – at the Mill House.* Ken is wearing his new officer's attire, and there is no mistaking 2nd Lt. Kenneth McDougall for the Boy Scout in the photo from Fort Bragg. There are no wrinkles in this uniform. He stands erect and broad shouldered, every inch the officer, relaxed in his new, confident persona. Less than a year after enlisting, the change is evident at a glance.

Kenneth – 1943 – at the Mill House

Mother in the gardens at 408 Swift Avenue, 1943.

Ken's days at home passed quickly, and all too soon he was on a train full of soldiers headed to Colorado. To his relief, the rumors of disarray in the mountain troops had turned out to be exaggerations and he was able to return to Camp Hale. Even with that good fortune, it was difficult to leave Durham. Once aboard the train, he barely fought back his tears and "just managed not to disgrace the infantry."

At Camp Hale, assigned now to the 86th Regiment, Ken worked in various Headquarters jobs before finally settling into F Company. This was what he had been waiting for, the reason for all the training at Fort Benning. He instructed a rock climbing class and found it rewarding work, but many parts of the job didn't come easily to him. Ken didn't like the idea of bending people to his will and preferred to do a job himself rather than forcing someone else to do it. In addition, he found it difficult to require his normally soft voice to shout a command loudly or gruffly enough. When he did manage, his mouth tended to turn up into a smile that he couldn't control.

It was in this summer of 1943 – July 27 to be exact – that Ken became an American citizen. The Army hauled about thirty men into the nearby town of Leadville, where a judge naturalized them in a simple ceremony. Ken sent Mother a postcard telling her why he was in Leadville and about a tour he had taken to learn how the mills extract gold, silver, copper, and lead from the earth. The card is beautiful, a picture of Colorado's state flower, the columbine, growing wild among aspen trees. Ken closes with the words,

*These flowers are a treasure that will outlast all the precious metals.*

*Yours, Ken, US citizen.*

On a lighter note, he told Mum that in spite of his naturalization, "The accent persists." In a later letter Ken was more introspective about the events of that day. He wrote his mother that American citizenship was the right and decent thing to do, given that he planned to spend his life in the United States. To his credit though, Ken admitted to having "an awful qualm while foreswearing allegiance to all foreign powers and potentates." He pointed out that his naturalization would make it easier for them to travel to England once the war ended, and said that he hoped they might be able to go as early as the next summer since, "The Nazis seem to be getting very short of planes."

Ken enjoyed the summer at Camp Hale. His company spent a lot of time on maneuvers, training in mountain fighting tactics. In their time off, Ken, Red, and Wilson continued their explorations, once going back to the site of their former Test Detachment camp.

The men stayed in a cabin near Aspen where Red taught them how to prepare decent meals out of army rations. The three of them "walked up to the old camping place for old times' sake. The cows were back in the meadow, and the chipmunks still played about the stone foundations we built last summer with so much labor. The beavers had quite restored their ponds to order, and even the one wooden hut we had left was being gradually destroyed by hungry porcupines. We all felt quite sentimental about the place and vowed to spend another holiday there after the war." Ken told Mother that he hoped she, too, would see it someday.

That same summer, the 10th Mountain Division found itself with an overage of junior officers. Quite a few men had to be transferred out of the division, and a number of those weeded out were married. Many of them had already uprooted their wives and children and moved them to Colorado. A group of single officers volunteered to leave Camp Hale in place of those men, allowing their married colleagues to remain with their families.

On September 11, 1943, Ken transferred out of the 10th Mountain Infantry Division with a group of friends, including Bill Merritt, a Wesleyan graduate from Rhode Island. Gregarious and easy-going, Bill was a popular officer who shared Ken's passion for good books.

The men all carried identical orders allowing each of them a ten-day leave before reporting to a base near Washington, D.C. Ken spent this time in Durham with Mother and Mum. He gardened, hiked, and did minor household repairs, sprucing up 408 Swift Avenue and getting everything in good order. The night before his departure, Mother and Mum gave a surprise going away party, packing the house with friends and neighbors. Although Ken had no specific orders to ship out, everyone knew that he would be going overseas very soon.

It was a distraught Mother who saw Ken off at the railroad depot the next morning. She gave him a gift as he climbed aboard his train, a pocket-sized edition of the New Testament. The Bibles, commonly given to men going overseas, carried an inspirational message from

Bill Merritt, 1942
*Photo courtesy of Jim McHutchison.*

President Roosevelt typed on the flyleaf. Mother wrote her own loving vow on the inside cover:

*Dear Ken,*

*I send this little book to seal the promise I made to you to wait for you with love in my heart, and faithfulness in my actions.*

*Your Loving Pearl*

The letter thanking Mother for the Bible and saying that he would cherish it as much for her words as for the scriptures bore the return address of an officer's replacement depot in Fort Meade, Maryland. The next two letters she received, also postmarked Fort Meade, gave no clue to what Ken was doing and seemed stifled by the fact that there was not much he was allowed to write about. He said only that they were so busy that there was little time to brood over the lives they left behind, and that it was just as well. "That desperate empty feeling only gets worse with dwelling on it and can only be filled by being with you. There is really nothing to say but that I love you very much."

For years Mother and Ken had had an implicit understanding that someday they would marry, but they had never considered themselves formally engaged. On September 30, 1943, Ken made it official: he asked Mother to marry him. Although it would seem logical for him to have proposed in person, the two of them having just been together, his proposal must have coincided with orders to ship out and the sense of immediacy that those orders aroused. He wrote, "It will be some time before we meet again."

But it could be that shy Ken simply chose to take this important step on paper. He was fond of saying that the best thing about a letter was that you could say things on paper you could not say so easily in person. The bad part, according to Ken, was waiting for a reply. And wait he did, because before he received Mother's answer, Ken was on a troop ship bound for North Africa.

It took some time for Mother's response to reach Ken – so long that he proposed a second time. He never had any doubt about what her answer would be, but told her that he wanted to ask again because, "There is a great satisfaction in the mere words!"

The day Ken received Mother's letter accepting his proposal, he immediately wrote her a long letter saying, "I know you wanted us to be married some time ago, but I was against it then…with the war on it was different…Marriage is more than a ceremony. When you and I get married you won't find us on opposite sides of the world. I shall kiss you on the mouth at sunset and on the forehead every dawn. And in the hours between I shall kiss you all over your body until we become like one person instead of two. In the day time you shall see much of me, for I shall never be far away.

"When we have a child, it will be our child, for I intend to have as much of a hand in it as nature will allow. I shall love it as much as you will, and almost as much as I love you. And the next one will be just as welcome and the one after that too.

"I don't know how much money we shall have, but we will have something over our heads and something growing outside of it. We will make ourselves a circle of happiness that will be the envy of the world."

# VI.

*I love thee to the level of everyday's*
*Most quiet need,*

The first letters Ken wrote after he shipped out let Mother know that he was somewhere in North Africa. Regulations prohibited his telling her exactly where he was. Unable to write about specifics, he described his general surroundings beginning with the Atlantic crossing.

Ken had made many ocean voyages in the years after his family immigrated to the United States, but the three-week crossing in October of 1943 was under unique circumstances. He was going to war this time, sailing toward an uncertain future. The possibility he might never return heightened his appreciation for everything he saw – "The sea itself, and the tremendous dome of sky, put on their never ending show of color and movement," and to Ken's eyes they had never been bluer or more beautiful. The troop ship was crowded and uncomfortable, but he wasn't one to be concerned about accommodations. He spent most of his time on deck and found the ocean remarkably calm.

By day, Ken watched for porpoises, whales, sharks, and flying fish. When it grew dark, he noted the similarities between the constellations overhead and the familiar stars in the sky over North Carolina, telling Mother, "You must have noticed the wonderful display of stars and planets in the early morning sky. Venus is brightest and nearest to the sun. I take her for a good omen. Jupiter is nearby, Saturn and Mars higher up in the sky. From this latitude we can see a little more of the southern sky than you can in North Carolina, though not much...I am learning some new constellations and how to tell north from any part of the sky that may be visible."

When Ken's ship docked in North Africa, the Army assigned him to a replacement depot, one of the dreary holding centers for reinforcements. No one wanted to be in such a place. Men in the depots awaited the call to fill a vacant slot in some depleted regiment, replacing a dead or wounded soldier. There was a general feeling among the men that the Army regarded replacements as little more than cannon fodder.

Ken had a platoon assigned to him from time to time, but it was only for organizational purposes; they weren't going into combat together. Still, the responsibility weighed heavily on him and he took his charge seriously, referring to himself as "Father of fifty, that's me."

The majority of men in Ken's platoon needed someone to look after them. Most had never been outside the United States, many never out of their home state. These men boarded a ship and crossed an ocean only to be dropped off in a land far removed from all they knew, prompting Ken to observe, "It is a wonderful experience for these American boys to see how the rest of the world lives, and believe me their eyes are popping."

When he signed passes for his men to leave the compound for a night out, Ken worried about them like a mother hen, fearful that someone might stab one of them or knock one over the head in a robbery. It was always a relief when they all showed up for roll call the following morning.

Ken began his North African campaign in Casablanca, Morocco, though he couldn't say so at the time, then moved on to Oran in Algeria. Surprised to find North Africa so lush and interesting, he wrote of its beautiful fields of lavender, telling Mother there must surely be lavender in the garden they would have someday.

He saw other fields – moors he called them – purpled by the same "bonny bell heather" found in his beloved Scottish highlands. He enclosed a sprig of heather in a letter, showing Mother the beautiful flower and telling her that it was the emblem of clan McDougall.

Ken had seen another part of Africa when his family passed through the Suez Canal on their world tour. Although Algeria's topography differed dramatically from the landscape he had observed then, some things reminded him of that earlier trip. Outside the army compound, everything was purely African, populated by a "weird and wonderful assortment of humanity" whose most obvious characteristics were "color, variety, and dirt." Scores of people clogged the roads with their carts, trucks, jeeps, wagons, bicycles, camels, horses, donkeys, cows, and goats. Anything that could roll or walk, laden to an impossible extent, teetered along until it collapsed.

Fascinated to find Arabs still living as they had before Roman times, Ken described houses with grass roofs and walls of sun-baked bricks or mud and wattle. He often came across nomadic shepherd tribes dressed in hooded, sack-like garb made of wool or goat hair, but he noted that the more well-to-do tribesmen wore robes and turbans of magnificent colors.

Ken took advantage of every opportunity to absorb the local culture. He admired an intricate design he saw in a museum, sketched the pattern onto a scrap of paper, and later duplicated it on a spoon he whittled for Mum. He mailed the gift to Durham along with a little buckle he carved for Mother out of a piece of gypsum.

Knowing that he had to allow six weeks or more for a package from North Africa to reach the United States, Ken mailed Mother's Christmas gifts in October. He bought her a beautiful ivory necklace, its beads carved into complex, lacey designs. The beads, small near the clasp, grew progressively larger until they came together on either side of a triangular pendant. Inside the triangle, the artist had carved an elephant.

The ivory necklace was one of two gifts that Ken sent Mother for Christmas, 1943. He had finally finished something he had been laboring over for quite some time. Back in his Aspen days, Ken had passed the long hours of night watch whittling something for Mother by the light of a campfire. He told her, "This gift represents many happy hours of whittling and long thoughts of you and home."

In his talented hands, one of the Army's old oak tent pegs had become a chain of wooden links. Carved to interlock, each link joined the next without benefit of glue or mechanical means. The two ends of the chain converged at a rounded wooden heart carved from a piece of ammunition box. The heart, about an inch thick, measured about three inches across at its widest point.

Ken had carved a keyhole into the center of the heart and then had whittled a key to fit the hole. He sent Mother the heart to wear around her neck, and he wore the key around his own, intending that someday the heart and the key, like the two of them, would be together again.

Until that time came, Ken determined to make the best of his situation. He explored his new surroundings and wrote Mother long letters describing the exotic places he saw.

"Today is Sunday and I have just come back from a long walk… The sun was very warm and the sea very blue. Small lizards sunning themselves on the wall scurried along to their private crannies as I came by. A fox barked on the hill…the fields were yellow with wild mustard that sent a sweet perfume across the countryside.

"Dark, shiny-leafed orange trees are illuminated by great clusters of their own golden fruit. Pomegranates are full sized but still green. They have a squarish look about them.

"It was one of those windy days with great cloud masses sailing by. I love to watch the fields change color as the cloud shadows race across them. The yellow mustard still looked like sunshine, even in the shade, but the green grass, the red earth, and the purple heather glowed or faded with the changing light in perpetual succession. Far away were blue mountains and a great arm of the sea reaching back into the land. Across the bay to the west the hills cut a knife-sharp line across the sunset sky.

"Now, the moon is riding high in the east…Oh, this big, round African moon. How we could enjoy it!"

Impressed with the beauty of Algeria, Ken included it, along with the Colorado Rockies and the Pacific Northwest, on the list of destinations he wanted to revisit in his post-war travels with Mother.

It was on the beaches of North Africa that Ken began to appreciate his broad scientific education. Taken aback to find grown men afraid of starfish and sea cucumbers, he soon realized that the majority of men couldn't identify even the most common ocean creatures. Still more astounding to Ken was the men's lack of interest or even curiosity about the things they saw.

His own eyes missed little, affording him an abundance of interesting things to examine. He spotted limestone cliffs and noted that the cliff sides were full of fossil worm tubes, fossil shells, and fossilized barnacles the size of his fist. He spent an afternoon digging them out of the cliff walls, intending to send the more interesting specimens to Dr. Pearse, his mentor in Duke's zoology department. He dug until it was nearly dark and then trudged back to camp with pockets bulging and helmet overflowing.

Carrying fossils was only one of many uses Ken found for his heavy, dark green helmet. In his first experience as a soldier in the field, he grew dependent on his helmet and wondered how men in the First World War ever managed to get along with their "flat tin hats." Ken found a great number of uses for the deeper World War II version.

"At the moment my helmet is doing duty as a candlestick. At night it hangs at the bed head and holds pipe and tobacco and the normal contents of my pockets. During the day I use it as a wash basin to shave and wash in, as a laundry tub, and as a seat. It is grand for collecting shells and things or carrying packages from the PX. The liner is a good storage place for a certain kind of paper. And last but not least, it is a very comfortable hat that keeps the rain and sun off – and other things perhaps. I couldn't do without it at all."

Ken traveled east across North Africa, transferred from one replacement depot to another, shifted among companies and battalions within the depots. Like so many men, he went long periods without receiving mail, a common problem for soldiers who did not have a permanent address. Ken found the lack of mail, or more specifically, the Army's inability to get his mail to him, the most depressing and demoralizing aspect of his time in the service.

Men passed their days in the depots as best they could. They read or played cards, chess, or various athletic games, but mostly they talked, usually about plans for life after the war. When they wore out that topic, the conversation generally shifted to food.

Food held a peculiar fascination for soldiers living on field rations. The Thanksgiving meal of 1943 was a good example of its importance in their lives. Far from home and missing their loved ones, men eagerly awaited the holiday. For weeks beforehand, they reminisced about family dinners they had enjoyed over the years, relishing the warm memories those past celebrations brought to mind.

On Thanksgiving Day, the soldiers came together on a hillside full of old olive trees. The site overlooked a vast plain with mountains rising in the distance. There had been heavy fighting in the area before the Allies pushed Rommel out of Africa. The ground, pockmarked with shell holes, was a virtual graveyard of war machinery. Wrecked tanks and jeeps, burned-out trucks, and the remnants of crashed airplanes lay all about. In the midst of this destruction, troops gathered for the quintessential American meal, and Ken found the food surprisingly good. Afterward he censored 800 letters and was amused to find that not one "failed to mention the turkey."

Ken had his own culinary memories to focus on. He asked Mum to teach Mother to make one of his favorite dishes, steak and kidney pudding. He spent long evenings amusing himself by planning how he and Mother would live after the war, and her ability to prepare such a meal was an essential element in his fantasy.

There was plenty of time to attend to such minutiae; Ken had little else to do. It got dark early in North Africa, often by six o'clock, and frequently there were no candles available to provide light for reading or other activities. On those occasions Ken would go to bed and lie awake for hours thinking about his future with Mother. Both of them were avid readers, and he loved to dream of the library they would have someday, "and all the good books that will be on the shelves for us and our children to enjoy."

When he could find a candle, Ken spent his evenings writing long letters updating Mother on his plans for the future: The fun they would have, the places they would go, what would grow in their garden. He submitted all his ideas for her approval, but everything he mentioned pleased her. Spending her life with Ken was the only thing that mattered to Mother, and she told him, "I shall really ask very little of this world if I can just have you to love me. And how I shall love loving you! You can even name the children! We must have at least four or five."

Thinking about names for the children he and Mother hoped to have was one of Ken's favorite pastimes. He suggested the name Mary for their first daughter, saying that he thought it went well with McDougall and he liked the fact that it couldn't "be easily abbreviated into some ugly nickname." He also proposed naming a daughter Janet in memory of his beloved little sister.

Mother was doing her share of planning and dreaming, too. She shopped for her own engagement ring, and unorthodox though it was, it pleased them both.  She chose a moonstone, not a surprising choice considering that the moon held such special significance for them.

An inexpensive stone bearing a vague resemblance to an opal, moonstones reflect light with a glow not unlike the luminescence of moonlight.  Mother told Ken that she chose the stone because it signified great lovers.  He replied that he didn't know if they would qualify on that account, but he knew their love would be constant and that was more important.

She described the ring in detail, explaining how the gold band wrapped around her finger and then swirled into a loop around the stone.  Delighted that Mother had found a ring she liked, Ken wrote, "It sounds good.  What do sales clerks know about it anyway?  Diamonds may be the convention, but they are cold, glittery things at best.  Much better a stone that you can read the future in, as you have already done so surely.  You couldn't see the date in it could you?  Was it 1944?"

By the time Ken arrived in Casablanca in the fall of 1943, the tide of the war had begun to turn in favor of the Allies.  Five months earlier, on May 13, Axis forces had surrendered North Africa, and the battlefront had moved on to Sicily and then the Italian peninsula.  Each Allied victory raised hopes that the war would soon be over.  Like every other soldier, Ken eagerly anticipated going home.

He and Mother began to plan their honeymoon, initially deciding to go to the Smoky Mountains but later discussing other possibilities. If they married in September or October, Ken thought they should honeymoon in New Hampshire.  He vividly recalled the resplendent New England autumns he had known as a teenager and thought fall in New Hampshire one of the great wonders of the world.

Fall was Ken and Mother's favorite time of year; October their favorite month.  They especially loved October in the mountains when the air became crisp and the trees put on their brilliant show of color. Mother spoke of wanting an October wedding, and Ken told her that was fine if that was when he returned to Durham.  If he came home any other month – even September – he said he could not possibly wait until October to marry.

Where they honeymooned concerned Ken less than that they marry as soon as possible.  He even suggested shortening the wait by having Mother meet him in England at war's end so they could honeymoon in the British Isles. That way they could marry as soon as Germany surrendered.

Ken felt that the war was the only thing standing between the two of them, and he thought it had cost them enough time already. Once he and Mother reunited, there was nothing more important to him than that they marry and begin their life together.

But while the two of them waited anxiously for the war to end, Ken languished in replacement depots. With little else to occupy him, he volunteered to instruct some of the numerous classes. Surprisingly, he found that he was becoming a soldier at last. He actually enjoyed lecturing and conducting calisthenics or drills. A teacher at heart, Ken finally had an opportunity to do what he was so well qualified for and to develop his own style. He discovered "how to be tough without being mean" and wrote, "The men seem to appreciate it. The change first became apparent when I found myself getting disgusted with the way some officers do these things, and realizing that I could do them much better myself. It was that that gave me the self confidence that was so painfully lacking at first."

As Ken traveled across North Africa, moving ever closer to the fighting in Italy, he found the journey increasingly agonizing. The Army relied on the French rail system for transportation, and it was rife with problems. Chief among Ken's complaints was the fact that the trains were primarily "40 and 8" boxcars left from WWI. The cars had held forty Frenchmen or eight horses in the previous war. The Americans could pack in no more than thirty men, and when they lay down to sleep they overlapped uncomfortably.

Worse, the trains were filthy. There were no toilets in the boxcars and no reliable source of safe drinking water. Steam or electric engines powered some trains, but most burned coal and emitted a thick black smoke that covered everyone and everything with a greasy grit.

Even more infuriating was the way the system operated. Ken estimated that the train moved slowly two thirds of the time and didn't move at all the remaining third. Every time the train pulled to a halt, men poured out of the cars to stretch their legs, barter for souvenirs, or check the local canteens for food. No sooner would they alight than with little warning the train would start up again, causing everyone to race back and throw themselves aboard. Often they found that it was a false start – or one of many false starts – and the whole process repeated itself.

It was a frustrating way to travel, but then Ken found almost everything about his situation exasperating. He was baked by the sun or blasted by sand storms one day; the next day brought torrential rain and mud up to his ankles. Grit or mud covered everything he owned. Food blew off his plate when he tried to eat, and his tent almost washed down a hillside while he slept. It seemed to him that his situation only got worse the further east he went.

By late November of 1943, Ken was in a place he identified only as being far from Oran. He was most likely in Tunisia then; by early December he had moved on to southern Italy.

Italy's situation in World War II was complex. Initially it was a member of the Axis powers, but in July of 1943 a palace revolt overthrew the fascist dictator Benito Mussolini. Authorities arrested Mussolini and held him prisoner at a hotel in Italy's Abruzzi region. Marshal Badoglio restored the pre-fascist system of government, and in September he signed both an armistice and an acceptance of unconditional surrender with the Allies.

Hitler had anticipated such an eventuality after Mussolini's downfall and had prepared for it by moving troops into northern Italy and capturing Rome. The Nazis headquartered themselves there and rescued Mussolini, who was a particular favorite of Hitler.

Mussolini remained under German protection in occupied northern Italy although he never again held any real power. He regrouped his followers into the "fascist army" that fought alongside Hitler's troops.

In October 1943, a month after surrendering to the Allies, the Italian government under Badoglio declared war on Germany. The new government's troops, referred to as co-belligerents, fought with Allied Forces.

Many civilians in German-controlled northern Italy worked to aid the Allied cause as well. These Italians, known as partisans, gave the Nazis a great deal of trouble. Even so, what Churchill called the "soft underbelly of Europe" was not at all soft for the troops whose job it was to push the Germans out of Italy.

# VII.
## ...by sun and candlelight.

Shortly after he arrived in Italy, Ken managed to get out of the hated replacement depots. On January 1, 1944, he and his friend Bill Merritt landed a plumb assignment. The two had left Camp Hale for Fort Meade at the same time, and then made their way through the replacement depots of North Africa and Italy together. At 4:30 in the morning on New Year's Day, Ken and Bill awoke to gale force winds that threatened to rip their tent apart and orders to move out immediately.

"Bill Merritt and I packed our bags by the last half inch of candle and set out on our journey. It was a hectic day. An hour or two in an open truck left us pretty well frozen stiff. However, we got to "X" and filled out a lot of papers. Then a wild jeep ride to "Y" where we reported in again and scrounged a hot lunch.

"We made a few hasty notes from a map and started off again in another jeep. The roads were churned up by military traffic of every description. 'Jerry' had long ago destroyed every bridge and culvert, giving the engineers the trouble of rigging up temporary crossings. After a number of wrong turns and detours we at last arrived here, a little mountain town. The town square was littered with branches blown down by the wind, adding to the ruins and destruction left by the fighting.

"The door of the inn stood open. There was little reason to close it, for the rain fell just as heavily in the hallway as it did outside and the stone floor and stairs were green with moss.

"Three flights up we pried open a heavy door and found what we were looking for. The room was stone-floored and almost in darkness. Even a red-hot GI stove seemed hardly to take the chill off it. A major sat on an iron bed frame, blowing happily on a mouth organ. He was accompanied, with more vigor than rhythm, by a tiny drum in the hands of a lt. colonel. At a table two captains were playing cribbage by the light of a candle."

The cold, dark room at the top of the moss-covered stairs served as the command post for the Fifth Army's training program. Ken and Bill reported for duty as instructors at the Mountain Warfare Training School. High in the mountains of southern Italy, they were in the first of many villages they would call home.

After checking in and stowing their wet gear, Ken and Bill "threaded a mile of narrow alley-ways to the orphanage for chow," where they saw several familiar faces. They spotted Billy Sheldon, a friend from Camp Hale, sitting with Dick Whittemore, one of Ken's tentmates in the Aspen Detachment. Billy and Dick had left Colorado in December, part of the 10th Mountain Division's Mountain Training Group formed just a month earlier. The rest of the Division was still training stateside and would not join the war in Europe until early 1945, when they, too, would fight in Italy.

Dick and Billy introduced a third instructor, Ed Mueller. Ken and Bill enjoyed a hot meal and the chance to catch up on news from Camp Hale. Then, with the rest of the instructors, they "repaired to the Bishop's house for a good round of hot wine and songs. These Italians certainly can sing and lose no opportunity to do so."

Ken thoroughly enjoyed teaching mountain warfare classes. They often camped in the mountains, affording him a clear view of Mt. Vesuvius puffing away in the distance. He could say little about the purpose of their work, however. His letters allow only vague references to marching and hauling equipment up and down mountainsides.

Permitted to write about the more personal aspects of his life in Italy, he gave Mother long descriptions of his various residences, which ranged from campsites to the homes of local people. Ken, who appreciated quiet time alone, even found solace in an igloo for a time. Built as a demonstration, the igloo was so successful that he adopted it in an effort to get away from the officers' quarters, which was a two-room shack crammed with men.

There were about a dozen soldiers, American and Italian, assigned to the officers' quarters. Sleeping bags and equipment littered the floor of the ramshackle cabin, and wet clothing dripped from clotheslines that crisscrossed the rooms.

In the center of the larger room stood an old stove, and at night there was usually a pot of sweetened wine simmering on top. As mountain winds howled around the little shack, banging the shutters and making the whole building groan and shake, soldiers dipped into the pot. Shortly the stories and songs would begin, going on well into the night. Eventually the men would drift off to sleep, awakening at dawn to begin another day of classes.

As much as he enjoyed the camaraderie, the number of occupants grew until Ken yearned for peace and quiet. Although the temperature in the igloo hovered near freezing, its four-foot walls kept out both noise and wind. A stick thrust into the wall served as a closet. Twigs covered by straw and topped by a thick down-filled sleeping bag made a fine bed. Best of all, because the inside was purest white, a single candle lit the whole space brilliantly, giving Ken a quiet place to read and write.

The igloo was one of many interesting abodes during the winter of 1944. Billeted with groups of men, often quartered in abandoned houses and damaged buildings, Ken moved frequently, usually sharing accommodations with his friend Bill. The degree of comfort in their many homes varied greatly, with Ken describing their favorite residence as "warm as an ice box but clean and neat."

Located somewhere near Naples, this particular place still housed its owners, a kindly older couple. They offered Ken and Bill a lovely bedroom with red and white tiles on the floor and pale pink walls covered in religious hangings. A set of double doors led from the bedroom onto a large balcony overlooking the rocky gorge that divided the town. Across the gorge stood the Duke's palace with beautiful terraces of orange trees.

The balcony, also the location of Ken and Bill's private toilet nestled among pink geraniums, served as a meeting place for the instructors. There men would gather to talk, sing, drink wine, sing some more, and occasionally shoot an orange off one of the Duke's trees just to test their steadiness of hand. Ken wrote that life in the military was so bizarre that such activities had begun to seem perfectly normal.

The couple who owned the house were so happy to see Allied soldiers that they overlooked their hijinks. The old man and woman had been poorly treated by the German troops who previously occupied the town, and the grateful couple smothered Ken and Bill with kindness.

A good deal of their attention involved trying to make conversation. Although fluent in both French and German, Ken didn't consider himself accomplished in Italian, nor was he given to frivolous chitchat. But his relentless little landlord, armed with a tattered grammar book, wasn't easily dissuaded.

The scarcity of heating fuel aided the old man's friendly endeavors. There wasn't enough wood to build a roaring fire and not nearly enough charcoal to heat the entire house. To keep warm, everyone had to gather around the kitchen table with a pan of hot coals set at their feet. The charcoal put out the home's only heat with the tabletop trapping the warmth. Ken thought it an ingenious system, but dreaded the laborious and mostly one-sided conversations that ensued.

"They have just persuaded me to sit with them this evening...the trouble is that neither of them has a word of English, yet both insist upon talking to me all the time. At this moment he is thumbing through an ancient Italian grammar, cooking up some other wise remarks for my attention. Nothing can stop him."

Despite such minor inconveniences, Ken loved instructing at the Mountain Warfare School. He was doing the two things he loved best: teaching and climbing mountains.

When sent out alone on reconnaissance, Ken scaled the highest mountain in the region and described the magnificent vistas he witnessed. "What a view! Snow covered mountains in every direction. And in between, winding valleys with rivers, beech forests, and little villages. Some of the latter are perched on small hills or cling to the sides of steep mountains. This used to be great country for brigands and most of the villages were built with an eye to defense. The Germans have not been slow to take advantage of that fact."

As he climbed toward the summit, Ken encountered massive snow drifts, caves with icicles thirty feet long, and snow valleys so brilliant in the winter sunshine that he "half expected to see a flock of snow-griffins, or at least a beautiful princess in ermine and tights."

He wrote detailed letters from Italy describing everything he saw and did in his free time. Ken recounted the more mundane activities as thoroughly as the most exciting, never failing to see the humor in any situation.

"Today four of us toiled up to a monastery that is stuck on a ledge about a thousand feet above the town. There was snow on the ground up there – it seemed another world entirely, so quiet and still. A young Franciscan monk showed us around, not forgetting to demonstrate a sacred drop of blood in a little bottle. The war surged by this place, but I shouldn't wonder if these monks were not even aware of it.

"When we started down again the monk came with us. It seemed he was taking a donkey and a pig down to the market. At first the donkey started off bravely, but the pig absolutely refused to head downhill. It was just about as strong as the monk, so their tug-of-war was a tie. Then an idiot boy came up and started beating the pig with a stick. With ear-splitting squeals the pig took off like a shot from a gun, the monk tearing along behind on the other end of the string, his brown robes flying. They soon overtook us and the donkey too. At this point the donkey decided to turn around and go back. We persuaded him against it with some trouble, and finally the monk got hold of both his animals at once. With a stroke of something very like genius, he tied them to opposite ends of the same string, pig leading, donkey in the rear, and monk in the middle, throwing his weight this way or that according to the needs of the moment. In this way they got along famously, except that the pig objected to corners and tried to take a short cut for home at every turn in the trail. Here and there we passed a peasant woman gathering wood, each of whom would deliver a good whack on one of the three, whichever happened to be within range. Things went at a great rate till near the bottom of the hill, when the procession ran into six cows, two goats, two dogs and a boy. I didn't think any of us would come out of that alive. However, when the yelling and squealing died away, the cattle were scattered to the four winds and the pig, the monk and the donkey were still on their way to the market in good order… We all laughed so much we could hardly get home. I just wish you could have seen it all."

# VIII.

*I love thee freely,*

On January 1, 1944, the day Ken had reported to the Mountain Warfare School, Mother had begun four weeks of basic training with the Army Nurse Corps at Camp Rucker, Alabama. The letter she had written Ken telling him that she had enlisted took over two months to reach him in Italy. It was early February before Ken learned that she was in the Army.

Mother hadn't been able to join the military when the war began. She still suffered occasional back problems from a car wreck a few years earlier. Since her personal physician wouldn't give her a clean bill of health, she had put off enlisting, afraid that she would fail the required physical examination. Her conscience dictated that she do something related to the war effort, however, so she found work with the American Red Cross.

Throughout the early years of the war, the Red Cross recruited nurses for the Army Nurse Corps. Mother wasn't involved in that aspect, but her job teaching civilian first aid courses did offer one advantage: When rumors began circulating that the War Department had enough nurses and would soon cease recruiting, she was among the first to hear.

Mother didn't like teaching and feared she might miss her last chance to join the military. She gathered her courage and rushed to enlist. The dreaded physical turned out to be little more than a formality, and she passed easily. On December 7, 1943, two years to the day after the attack on Pearl Harbor, Mother swore her oath of allegiance.

Mother, front and center. Army Nurse Corps basic training at Camp Rucker, Alabama, 1944.

Women of the Army Nurse Corps entered the service as second lieutenants. As a new recruit, Mother had to participate in the Army's physical training exercises and learn to take orders and march in formation. As a new officer, she had to learn to give orders.

She hated giving orders. Agreeable and easy-going, Mother worried that people wouldn't like her if she went around barking out demands. Ken had experienced the same qualms early on and told her she needed to get past those feelings and "make 'em do it. You'll find the only ones who will dislike you for it are the ones who are not worth their salt anyway. Be just, be firm, and feelings will take care of themselves."

After Mother finished basic training, she stayed in Alabama and was assigned to Northington General Hospital in Tuscaloosa, a small town in the west central part of the state. She enjoyed her time at Northington, meeting new people and feeling she was making a vital contribution to the war effort. The Army also sent Jo Hawthorne to Tuscaloosa. Jo was one of Mother's closest friends, a former classmate at Duke Nursing School.

Patients at Northington were severely injured soldiers who had endured months in various hospitals overseas. Once they returned to the United States, the Army tried to place soldiers in facilities close to their homes so that family members could visit, but most men were still lonely. Days passed slowly in the hospital. After an hour or two in rehabilitation services or physical therapy, men had only board games or books to occupy their time.

Because there wasn't a lot for Jo and Mother to do on their time off, they made it a point to explore the small towns around Tuscaloosa. Often they invited a few of their more able-bodied patients to come along.

One of their favorite jaunts was to the nearby town of Eutaw, Alabama. About thirty miles from Tuscaloosa, Eutaw was a sleepy little town with a wealth of beautiful old houses, many dating from the previous century. Strolling Eutaw's shady streets, admiring the elegant homes and their lovely, well-maintained gardens, provided a soothing change of pace for the soldiers and a pleasant respite for Jo and Mother.

Ken was not thrilled to learn Mother was in the Army. Envious of the soldiers she and Jo took to Eutaw, he admitted to being fraught

Mother in uniform.

with jealousy having seen the "rush around" army nurses got. But he respected Mother's decision to enlist and thought that everyone benefited from leaving home and getting a broader view of the world.

He requested a picture of her in uniform and told her, "I am very proud of you – but I always was that.

"I do hope that you will like it, that all my advice was ill founded, and that you will find useful work and plenty of it. If they keep you hanging around with nothing much to do, don't let it get you down. Look at me. I've probably done no more than six days of useful work in nearly two years of army life. With a conscience like your's though, it will probably take about two years to develop that old 'What the hell do I care?' attitude.

"At least you are training to save lives, not take them. That is good.

"We shall have fun comparing notes after the war. Someday we shall sit on that little old bench above the Eno and begin all over again. But then the war will seem like a dream that is almost forgotten as soon as you wake up. Next time too, we shall know that we belong together and are going to stay together whatever comes. It will be a good feeling; it will always be with us."

It relieved Ken to know that Mother was serving stateside, comfortably out of harm's way. Mother, on the other hand, spent her days nursing seriously wounded soldiers. She was all too aware of the dangers that could befall Ken, and she grew more fearful about his safety with each passing day.

Ken had entered North Africa long after the fighting ended – the danger there had been relatively remote. There were still many battles ahead before the Allies could reclaim Nazi-occupied Italy, however, and Mother knew that he would see combat there. She begged him to be careful and told him, "I devour the newspapers and listen to the radio at every opportunity, just hoping each day that the big blow has hit home over there. The news seems very promising today, but as I have told you before, the war never loses any of its horror for me when I know that you are still in danger. Not until I feel your arms around me will I really smile again."

Ken reassured her that he was being cautious and tried to distract her by writing about the interesting things he did when he wasn't working. He visited Pompeii, a fascinating sight that his family had missed on their world tour, and he revisited Naples.

It distressed Ken to compare the Naples he saw in 1944 to the one he had seen with his family seventeen years earlier. Amazed to find the people as warm and friendly as he remembered from his first visit, Ken thought Italian children must be the most beautiful in the world. He told Mother that they looked like cherubs, "emaciated cherubs."

"Many years ago I walked through the narrow streets of Naples with crowds of ragged little children at my heels, begging for pennies. This time there were 200 soldiers behind me. The children were still there. They were raggeder, dirtier, thinner and more insistent than before and their parents were not above joining them. These people have suffered.

"You can hardly imagine the lengths they will go to get something to eat. Thank goodness the AMGOT (American Military Government of Occupied Territories) is already getting food to them, but the job can hardly be done adequately until the fighting is over. It is dreadful to think of the vast numbers of people in even worse straits than these, all over Europe. It will be a stupendous job to get them all back onto their feet."

During his stay in the mountains around Naples, Ken added the area to the list of places he wanted to show Mother someday. He told her, "It seems we shall have quite a lot of territory to cover, but then there are so many wonderful places in this old world… All the beautiful things I see – and there are many – seem to be wasted since you cannot see them too.

"Like you, I also have that uncomfortable sense of being only half a person. I quite regret all the good times I had before we met, because you can never really know about them now. We will go to new places and gradually build up a background for ourselves of experiences in common. Our wedding will be the birth of a new personality. Let's call him 'MacDoubrough.' You and I will gradually fade away (but, like old soldiers, never die!) as Mac becomes more and more distinct. We will expose him to all the good books and good music that he can afford. From you he will learn how to make many friends and how to love the good things of home. I will show him the mountains and the sea and what there is to see under a rotten log in the forest. I think he will enjoy life.

"I naturally want to get home and start our life together. But even that continual longing does not blind me to the many beauties of the places we go. It is a great little old world in its way. And I for one am never tired of looking it over."

Ken visited many places that because of censorship he could not name. But his words painted detailed images of tiny Italian villages stuck to the sides of mountains like swallows' nests, with stone structures barely distinguishable from the mountainside at a distance. Most houses had no glass in the windows, only wooden shutters to close against the elements.

He described village streets so steep that he almost needed a rope to climb them and so narrow that they could only be traversed single file. Ken told Mother that she would surely love these little towns, and he wanted to show them to her after the war.

For her thirty-second birthday, February 2, 1944, Ken sent a souvenir from one such town. "I found a tiny shop in a backstreet where an old man sat in the window, carving cameos. He was cutting a large seashell that is found along the African coast of the Mediterranean. The inner layer of these shells is red or brown, forming the background of the cameo. The middle layer is pure white, as you will see, and is left to form the figure. I am sending you an example of this old man's work, hoping it may arrive by Ground Hog's Day."

Ken chose a large cameo, the artist's detailed rendering of a chariot drawn by horses. The old man pinned his exquisite handiwork to a small blue cushion and then placed it in a sturdy box to protect it on the long trip to America.

In an effort to put Mother's mind at ease, Ken wrote about benign things, things he thought might be of interest to her. He described the birds he saw as they were both avid birdwatchers. Delighted to sight birds he hadn't seen since he left Scotland more than six years earlier, he told her, "I saw a robin sitting on an old stone wall. It was an English robin. No bigger than a sparrow, with russet coat and waistcoat of bright brick red. He had a cocky little eye, as they all do...Yesterday I heard a real English skylark singing. It was quite a shock to realize that you have never heard one."

He told Mother that he had seen a stork fly over and had cautioned the bird to be careful because soon it would have a job to do for the two of them. He detailed the loud and complicated courtship of some nearby magpies and mentioned hearing a cuckoo that brought back happy memories of birds he used to hear in the Scottish glens.

As Allied Forces readied for the coming invasion of Europe, emphasis shifted away from mountain fighting, and classes at the Mountain Warfare School began to dwindle. This afforded Ken and his fellow instructors more time to explore.

"We have been having a slack time lately and enjoying ourselves in a big way. I took off one day to explore a great gorge, or canyon, not far away. It is about a thousand feet deep and several miles long. It was quite a job getting down into it by following goat tracks down the cliffs. At the bottom a small stream rushed along between towering rock walls.

"As I made my way downstream the gorge opened out into a narrow green valley with sheep and goats grazing in it. Purple crocuses were in bloom everywhere and hazel catkins were already long and yellow.

"Presently there came a shout that echoed back and forth from the cliffs on either side: 'WHERE ARE YOU GOING JOHNNY?' All I could see was an immense pile of brush moving along on two very short human legs. It turned out to be a little old man, little more than a dwarf. When he dropped his load I saw two twinkly black eyes, a huge hooked nose, rosy red cheeks, and a fuzz of yellow beard. He continued to speak in a voice that seemed to shake the very mountains. He had lived in New York for twelve years, but was already forgetting the language, so much of his shouting was of no avail. I made out that he was seventy-four years old and, like everyone else hereabouts, intends to return to the States after the war. I left him shouting at his sheep and feeding them the brush that he had carried down the cliff for them."

As Ken hiked in the mountains near Naples, he noted that great sections of hillsides seemed to have trees of almost identical size and age. He found an explanation for this puzzling phenomenon when local people began burning charcoal. Intrigued by their work, he followed their activity for several days.

"The charcoal burners live far back in the mountains with their families. They build themselves temporary houses out of sticks, stone, and turf, often perched like swallows' nests on the steepest hillsides. They all seem to have large families and even the tiny tots help in the work. The first stage is to build a platform partly dug out of the hillside, partly built up with logs. Then they start felling trees and dragging them to the platform. Every tree is first cut into small pieces and even the finest twigs are used. After a week or two of continuous work, they have made a great pile of wood on the platform every stick of which is laid just so. The pile is covered over with leaf mold and earth and then lighted. It burns very slowly.

"For about a week, a tall column of white smoke pours out of it scenting the air for miles around. When it dies out they remove the earth covering and there is a great pile of precious charcoal. They shovel every last scrap of it into huge sacks which are strapped to mules and donkeys and carried down into the towns for sale.

"Then another platform is built and another tract of hillside is cleared. Where they have been working for a long time you can see whole mountainsides dotted with their old platforms. When the pace of work gets too far from home, they simply build a new home on one of the used platforms. It is an ingenious system. One of the good things about it is that they leave a sprinkling of young trees which later grow into valuable timber. Also, new growth springs up from the cut stumps, and in fifteen or twenty years they can cut another crop for charcoal."

It was fortunate that Ken found time to see so much of southern Italy because the Mountain Warfare School disbanded in February of 1944. All the instructors had to move on to other units.

Ken wrote that he was with a fine outfit, one that was not easy to get into – the First Special Service Force. "The 1st S.S.F. is a combined U.S.-Canadian force. It is a carefully picked, highly trained force and I am very lucky indeed to get into it. As a matter of fact, I am more or less on trial here at present, but should be assigned before too long if all goes well." Ken's friends Bill Merritt, Dick Whittemore, Billy Sheldon, and Ed Mueller joined the Force along with him.

The First Special Service Force, America's first modern-day Special Forces unit, was formed to provide the Allies with commandos capable of making lightening strikes into German-held territory. Made up of equal numbers of Canadian and American troops, the FSSF was sometimes referred to as the "North Americans." Upon its inception, the number of enlisted men and officers was equally divided between Canadians and Americans. After that, men garnered promotions strictly on merit; the Force made almost no concessions to nationality. Their integration was so complete that when the Force disbanded, many men were shocked to find that their best friends were citizens of a different country.

Although the FSSF wasn't a clandestine operation, few people knew of its existence. Unique in every way, the Force operated directly under the U.S. War Department. Everyone wore American uniforms with a shoulder patch that bore the names of both countries.

A volunteer unit, the men of the Force trained as paratroopers, explosives experts, mountain fighters, ski troops, and amphibious assault forces. They also mastered commando tactics involving hand-to-hand combat.

Because they were few in number and subjected to the most difficult and comprehensive training in the Army, the FSSF soon achieved an *esprit de corps* difficult to match in larger units.

One reason for the successful cohesion of so varied a group was that both Canadians and Americans thought they had the finest leader in the Army. Lieutenant Colonel Robert T. Frederick, the man chosen to formulate and command the First Special Service Force, was a fine soldier and a brilliant tactician, a man not given to swagger or bravado. A graduate of West Point, this handsome man's small stature and quiet demeanor belied his hard-driven nature.

Frederick was a leader who never asked his men to do anything he wouldn't do. There was nothing, however, that he wouldn't do. Although he rose to the rank of Major General, he was always in the thick of things once fighting began. This trait inspired an almost reverential loyalty in the men who served under him.

Believing that it was an officer's duty to lead from the front, Frederick led both figuratively and literally and required officers under his command to do the same. His nine wounds granted him the dubious distinction of being the most wounded general in the Army.

The FSSF first saw action in the Aleutian Islands in August of 1943, alongside several units from the 10th Mountain Infantry Division. Shipped to North Africa a few months later, they landed in Casablanca in early November, and by mid-November they were in Italy.

The Force began fighting in the mountains almost immediately, suffering great losses but successfully breaking through sections of the

German Winter Line that no other unit had been able to breach. In the two and a half years they existed, the FSSF never lost a battle or gave up an inch of ground.

# IX.
## ...as men strive for Right.

On February 2, 1944, the First Special Service Force moved onto the beachhead at Anzio, a coastal town about thirty miles south of Rome. Anzio had been a popular seaside resort since ancient times. For four months in 1944, however, the area around the town was one of the bloodiest battlefields of World War II.

The Allies held a narrow strip of land running along the Tyrrhenian Sea, a pocket about fifteen miles long and seven miles deep. The territory encompassed most of the former Pontine Marshes, the mosquito-infested swamp that lay between the sea and the foothills of the Lepini Mountains. A series of canals had drained the swampland leaving a swath of flat, almost barren farmland.

British and American forces had gone ashore at Anzio on January 22, 1944. A series of heated battles had soon ensued as German soldiers tried to push the Allied army back into the sea. The Allies fought tenaciously to maintain their small foothold. By the beginning of March, the worst of the battles had ended with both sides still occupying their original positions. Both German and Allied troops were exhausted, their ranks depleted from six weeks of hard fighting. No longer able to launch massive offenses, the two sides settled into a pattern of small, isolated strikes against each other.

It was in Anzio that Ken joined the First Special Service Force, arriving there the first week of March, just as the worst battles for the beachhead subsided. Initially assigned to Force Headquarters for orientation, Ken turned down the opportunity to be First Regiment's

Intelligence Officer. He had had enough of headquarters jobs and wanted to be in the field, living with a group of men and getting to know them. Ken drew a temporary assignment: acting Company Commander for Fifth Company, First Regiment.

Company Commander was a dangerous job in Frederick's army. Still, it was work Ken wanted to do. It would have been easy for him to have situated himself in any number of safe positions early in his military service. Some sort of government research would have been the best course of action from a purely professional standpoint, but he didn't want that. Although several of his Duke friends were working on new anti-malarial drugs, Ken said that if he had chosen that route, "It would always have been on my conscience that I had shirked the harder course. However unpleasant it may be at times, I cannot regret having joined the infantry. She is the 'Queen of Battles' all right, even in these days of planes, tanks and big guns."

He went on to say that he wanted to see what men went through in battle because "front line troops have a pride in themselves and a hardly concealed scorn for '4Fs' and the 'rear echelon' that no one else can really understand. I should not care to be an object of their scorn, either now or after the war. But more than that it is a chance to find oneself...I am finding out a lot about myself, and about other men."

Ken's first few days at Anzio were quiet, prompting him to write that it seemed like a boring place. "The country is flat as a pancake, with few trees and dull little farm houses scattered on it. We exchange shell fire, air raids and patrol raids with 'Jerry' but neither side is getting anywhere (at present) and it all seems a wretched waste of time. I suppose we should be thankful for the lull, but it does get monotonous.

"Our company inhabits a long earth bank on the edge of a field. It is just like a prairie dog colony. I stick my head out in the morning and the other heads pop up all down the row. One by one we come out into the open, stretch, walk about a bit, look at the sky. Presently the smoke goes up everywhere and the smell of breakfast drifts across the field. We do exercises, problems of one sort or another, clean our equipment, improve our dugouts, and play football or baseball sometimes.

"Every now and then there is a loud – BANG – as one of Jerry's shells goes overhead. He is not shooting at us so no one even looks up. Sometimes we can see a great fountain of earth where the shell hits.

More often the shells come over one horizon and disappear over the other with nothing to be seen. They are none of our business.

"At dusk, if there is no job on hand, we crawl back into our holes, cover the opening tight, and light up the candles for an hour or so of reading or talking. Sometime during the night there is sure to be a Jerry plane about, taking pictures or dropping a bomb or two. He doesn't dare to come over in the daylight. We seldom see him, but the guns roar from every hedgerow. They make a wonderful sound. Quick firing AA guns go 'room, room, room, room' till the very air seems to be rumbling on and on. If the plane comes lower the machine guns start barking out 'ack, ack, ack' in quick succession, dozens of them at once. Red tracer bullets go arching into the sky in long, flat, graceful curves. Shell bursts wink like huge red sparks among the stars. Then suddenly it all stops and there is dead silence, save for the earth shaking rumble and distant flashing of big guns far away."

Allied Forces at Anzio were woefully undermanned. It was the FSSF's responsibility to cover eight miles on the beachhead's right quadrant, about a fourth of the total Allied territory. Ken's company, as part of the Force's First Regiment, was responsible for the lower half of this area, land that ran alongside the Mussolini Canal all the way to the sea.

Although Allied Forces maintained a defensive line on the beachhead, in reality each side adopted an equal number of offensive and defensive techniques as they jockeyed for position in the area between them known as no-man's-land. Both Allies and Germans claimed territory by outposting in that zone – inhabiting the homes, barns, and outbuildings left empty when civilians evacuated. Depending on the location of the outpost it might house troops, or if situated far enough to the front it could be useful for spying.

Both armies sent parties of men to stake out buildings and demolition patrols to destroy any structure deemed useful to the enemy. On a daily basis, each side attempted to wipe out any gains in territory their opponents had made the previous night, and skirmishes often broke out when one or the other decided to claim a disputed outpost.

The First Special Service Force carried out nightly patrols across no-man's-land, sometimes venturing deep into German territory. Colonel Robert Moore commanded the Force's Second Regiment troops, the men who conducted the majority of the patrols. When Ken entered the FSSF, he trained under the "utterly fearless" Colonel Moore and wrote of participating in his first patrol.

"We were like a lot of thugs sneaking along the hedgerows in the moonlight. We had blackened our hands and faces, wore our oldest clothes, and carried rifles, knives, and hand grenades in our pockets. Quite suddenly we were fired on by a machine gun near a house, quite close. One man was shot in the leg. We ducked behind a bank and another gun opened up from that side. A flare went up and we squeezed ourselves against the ground, holding our breath till it burnt out. Mortar shells started to burst around us, the shrapnel whining overhead like angry bees. We scrambled back along the ditch and got away from all that. We next made a wide detour and started along a ditch across a field but someone could see us as shells started coming over 's-s-s-s-BANG! – s-s-s-s-BANG!' The ditch was full of muddy water but we got right down in it on our bellies and wriggled away from there like worms on a hot brick.

"Later that night we stalked along the bank of a flooded canal, among pine trees. It was very muddy and water in the ditch came well above our knees. There were birds in the marsh, bitterns perhaps, which sounded just like people talking quietly. It stopped us several times, finger on the trigger. Once we were stopped like that, crouched, listening, when I saw a man walking towards us in the shadows. We kept quite still and he came quite close, then stopped, listening, and looking straight at us. For at least a minute there wasn't a sound or a movement. I could think of nothing to say that seemed appropriate. Someone said, 'Hands up!' The man put up his hands and said, 'I'm English.' And he said it with a Scots accent that you could cut with a knife. He had been taken prisoner by the Germans and was coming back through our lines.

"We went back still further and tried a detour on the other side. But we were seen again and mortar shells came crashing down close by. They scared up a whole flock of Pee-wits that flew off in the moonlight crying their strange cry. Every now and then one of those shells went 'BANG!' overhead and set the sky to rumbling as it whistled away over the horizon. It was all very exciting and strange. I was surprised to find that I was not particularly scared."

Unlike the patrol Ken described, the First Special Service Force usually operated undetected. With their faces and hands blackened, Forcemen crept silently through the night on deadly combat patrols, earning them the nickname *Black Devils*. Often the enemy knew of their presence only after the fact, when they awoke to find their sentries dead, the FSSF calling card stuck on their foreheads or jacket lapels.

The Force calling card was a small square of white paper emblazoned with their symbol – a red Indian spearhead. Printed in white across the tip of the spearhead were the letters USA, with Canada printed vertically down the spine. Just to the right of the spearhead was a message written in German: *DAS DICKE ENDE KOMMT NOCH!* (Loosely translated as "The worst is yet to come!") Forcemen used the stickers liberally, slapping them onto fences, outpost buildings, and bodies.

Men of the Force, who called themselves *Braves*, were formidable opponents. They continually infiltrated German lines, pushing their defensive front forward outpost by outpost, holding their sector of the beachhead against incredible odds. When captured, they gave up almost no information and the Germans couldn't figure out how large the Force actually was. They concluded that the FSSF consisted of one, possibly two, divisions with the understanding that a division contained approximately 15,000 men. In fact, there were never more than 2,800 members of the FSSF active at any one time.

Like other Forcemen at Anzio, Ken lived in bombed-out buildings and holes in the ground, usually surrounded by the smell of dead soldiers, civilians, and animals. Although someone eventually came along and buried the human bodies, dead animals littered the countryside. Deer, cows, oxen, and horses often got caught in crossfire when fighting broke out or stepped on landmines as they grazed. Even cats and dogs wandering across fields sometimes detonated mines. The stench of rotting flesh was a constant on the beachhead.

If crossfire or exploding mines didn't kill any animals, there was always the errant shell or mislaid bomb. In the four months that the Allies held the beachhead, it was under continuous assault from both air and ground artillery.

Germans held the hills overlooking Anzio, giving them clear aim at Allied forces below. They bombarded the Allies daily with their most feared weapon, the deadly accurate cannons known as 88s. In addition they fired Nebelweffers, six-barreled rocket launchers nicknamed "Screaming Meemies" because of the sounds they made in flight. Nebelweffers weren't as accurate as 88s, but their piercing screech had a terrible psychological effect on the men.

There were also two huge railway guns known as Anzio Annie and the Anzio Express embedded in the hills above the beachhead. Their shells sounded like freight trains passing overhead.

The Luftwaffe pounded the Allies every night on quick bombing runs out of Rome, a mere twenty or thirty miles away. Allied planes made a much longer flight up from bases in southern Italy laden with heavy bombs to drop behind German lines.

Along with shells exploding and bombs dropping from the sky, there were frequent bursts of gunfire on the beachhead as one side or the other spotted patrols trying to sneak through their lines. Ken's first letters from Anzio mention that things were so quiet some days that it was almost possible to forget there were Germans nearby, but that most days – and every night – popped with noise.

He described how he and his men slept with their boots on, "and with pistols and helmets within reach. Seldom a night passes but Jerry drops some bombs around, or sends some shells over, or someone starts shooting, or 'things' are seen moving out in front of the wire. At every alarm we jump up, grab our guns, and try to find out what is going to happen next and what has to be done to meet it."

Evenings in Anzio, Ken said, held a special quality: They were "full of anticipation. Will it be a cloudy night, good for Jerry to creep up close without being seen? Will it be clear and moonlit, good for an air raid? Will it be warm or cold tonight, wet or fine? It makes so much difference."

Where a soldier bedded down for the night made a tremendous difference as well. Ken lived in a series of dugouts and outposts at Anzio, but his favorite quarters had been on the beach a few yards from the water. For a short while, he and a Canadian officer had occupied a cave-like hole about six feet long and five feet deep, lined with straw.

They felt safe at first. The shoreline on their part of the beachhead was of little significance to the Germans and unlikely to be bombed. But when waves breaking on shore grew loud enough to mask the sound of enemy troops sneaking up on them in the darkness, the men thought better of their situation and moved inland.

Ken had loved living on the beach, describing it as a "very pleasant sandy shore, though you never knew what the waves were going to wash in next. It would be a case of navy beans one tide, a dead horse the next.

"Only the sea itself seems impervious to the filth and destruction of war, which it spews out on the beaches or swallows up into its depths. What horrible messes we humans do make on the face of this green earth. No other animal treats it with such contempt."

# X.

*I love thee purely,*

Anzio was infamous. It received almost daily news coverage, and the articles troubled Mother. Ken tried to calm her fears by downplaying the hazards, but in truth Anzio was a dangerous place. Although Ken's position put him as far as possible from the prime targets – the harbor and the airstrip – there was no safe area. The beachhead was too small and exposed to offer much in the way of protection.

If Ken's reassurances made Mother feel better, it wasn't long before another news story rekindled her fears. The renowned war correspondent Ernie Pyle visited Anzio and filed reports that caused her a great deal of consternation. Ken assured her that the articles were only representative of the small areas Pyle visited, reminding her that reporters only went places where there was action. He pointed out that on his part of the front there was nothing much to write about, saying that the really exciting stories were actually isolated incidents. "The picture one gets of war from books, newspapers, and even from first hand accounts is surprisingly false…Even when there is a sharp engagement with many casualties, it always turns out that most of the casualties are merely wounded, and many of them are back on the job after a few weeks in hospital."

Ken didn't think Pyle's readers would be interested in hearing how he spent the majority of his time. Like all officers, Ken faced a myriad of problems every day, ranging from supply difficulties and paperwork to squabbles among the men, some of whom had been at the front so long, Ken said, that they were "half way back to nature already. They must be driven and wheedled to wash themselves and their clothes, to shave, to dig latrines and garbage pits, to keep the area free of trash, to purify the water with tablets, and above all, to take their pills, vitamin and Atabrine." Mosquitoes proliferated on Anzio's reclaimed swampland. Even so, men avoided the anti-malarial Atabrine because it made them ill and turned their skin a sickly, yellow hue.

At the end of a long day of dealing with such issues, Ken had to spend his evenings censoring the enlisted men's mail.

Shortly after Ken took over Fifth Company, Forceman Noe Salinas came to him with a problem. Noe's grandmother couldn't read English, so he had to write to her in Spanish. Finding an officer to censor the letters had always been difficult. To his relief, Noe found that Ken could censor letters written in Spanish as easily as he could those written in English.

A big Texan, Noe liked his new commander's ways and appreciated the fact that Ken hadn't imposed a lot of changes when he took over the unit. He had impressed Noe by taking the time to study the men serving under him to observe how they usually did things. Both quiet loners, Ken and Noe worked well together, with Noe often scouting for Ken on patrols.

Some of Fifth Company's other enlisted men had decided that their new Company Commander was a bit eccentric. They liked Ken, but they didn't understand his fascination with plants, insects, and marine life. They were unaware that their commanding officer was a veterinarian and a zoologist, facts that would have explained the behavior that they considered odd.

Ken's men didn't know about his background because he didn't tell them. Only his closest friends knew about his impressive education and his famous father. Ed Mueller once said that one of the things he most admired about Ken was that, "Although 'somebody,' he didn't talk much about himself."

Around seventy men served under Ken in Fifth Company, but in truth many of those soldiers were just boys, some not yet out of their teens. Their various troubles and concerns gave any officer more than enough to deal with, and handling the more recalcitrant among them required some ingenuity.

Jordan Markson tested Ken's ability. A feisty nineteen-year-old, Jordan quickly figured out that his situation couldn't get much worse. In addition to living in a hole in the ground and being shot at, he held the lowest rank. He rebelled against the rules he saw as ridiculous and remained oblivious to officers' threats – the primary threat being jail. Since men in jail weren't usually shot at, Jordan considered it a step up from his present position, or at the very least, no worse. Given his plight, he felt that his superiors had little leverage, wondering what more they could *possibly* do to him.

What Ken did was promote him. He called Jordan into Headquarters, where Jordan found Ken sitting behind a desk, his elbow resting on the desktop, a pair of sergeant's stripes lying in the open palm of his hand.

"Markson," Ken said with a smile, "we finally have something we can take away from you."

Ernie Pyle's readers wouldn't have found an officer's petty problems very interesting, and they certainly wouldn't have wanted to hear about the endless housekeeping chores at Anzio. As the front line moved forward one crumbling outpost building at a time, Ken despaired of ever being able to make any real improvement in his living situation. The places he called home were frequently nothing more than a few walls left standing, often with the roof blown off and the windows broken out. No sooner would he get the stench and filth under control in one outpost than he would have to leave.

"Having got our house almost fit to live in, we have now had to move to another, which is even filthier. How I loathe the battered houses and all the filth and wreckage that collects in and around them. Rats, mice, fleas, bedbugs, lice, 'crabs,' and cockroaches flourish everywhere, not to mention flies and mosquitoes. I wish we could move out and leave them all behind. Maybe they would attack the Germans and drive them out of Italy.

"I can't begin to describe the accumulation of old equipment, boxes and cupboards full of half-eaten food, dirty old dishes and pans, chests and bureaus full of old rags, horrible old mattresses full of bed bugs and fleas, floors ankle deep in rubbish, dust, and fallen plaster. Under one bed the chamber pot was cemented to the floor by a large pool of dried up blood.

"Round the house, outside, it is worse yet. Dead animals only half buried, latrines open and swarming with flies, mountains of garbage, tin cans and cardboard boxes."

In one outpost, someone left behind a few old chairs and an iron bedstead too worthless or heavy to lug away. The find delighted Ken. The chairs had no seats, so he wove coverings out of old telephone field wire and then stacked ration boxes to create a makeshift table. He improvised a bed by placing a door across the iron frame. The bed was a particularly treasured find as it allowed him to sleep a few inches above the filthy floor, affording some protection from the rats that crawled over everything at night.

Ken longed to be clean and swore that after the war he would never be dirty again. He read about a form of insanity where people were unable to stop washing themselves and feared he might be coming down with it.

He wasn't alone in feeling the strain of life on the beachhead. Everyone at Anzio lived under tremendous pressure. Unlike other fronts which had rest areas far behind the action, Anzio offered no safe place for battle-weary men to escape. There wasn't anywhere a soldier could effectively get off the front line for a few days. With the ocean to their back and the enemy fanned out in front, men had nowhere to go, no respite from the stress. The Germans joked that Anzio was the largest self-sustaining POW camp in Europe. Many men broke under the strain of constant bombardment, giving Anzio one of the highest psychological casualty rates of the war.

Even the field and evacuation hospitals on the beachhead offered a poor place to convalesce. The medical compound was the victim of so many attacks that it was nicknamed "Hell's Half Acre." Men doctored their minor wounds just to avoid going there. Soldiers who might have relished time to rest and heal in another hospital couldn't get out of Anzio's wards fast enough. With bullets and shell fragments zinging through the canvas walls of hospital tents, shattering plasma bottles and knocking equipment off tables, men felt safer in foxholes back on the line. No one wanted to be in a tent when the nightly shelling commenced.

Combat veterans often say that shelling is one of the most traumatizing aspects of war. The terrifying sounds, deafening noise level, shaking earth, and very randomness of the casualties take their toll physically and psychologically.

Ken wrote about one particularly heavy shelling when he lay in his dugout pressing his body into the ground for protection. Beneath him, the earth rumbled and rolled so violently that soil shook loose from the sides of his hole, matting his hair and seeping into his clothes. His ears rang from the concussion of the guns.

Just when he thought he couldn't withstand the shelling for another moment, Ken realized that he could hear a nightingale singing. At first, he thought he was imagining it, that it couldn't be happening. But the little bird was close by, its clear, sweet notes unmistakable through the sound of shells exploding all around. Ken couldn't believe the nightingale was not shaken from its perch by the blasts, but throughout the attack the bird never stopped singing.

The "most beautiful of all birdsongs" to Ken, the serene warbling brought back memories of nightingales heard years before during happy times. As he hugged the rolling earth, dirt sifting down onto his face, Ken wept at the beauty of the sound and the memories the little bird's song brought to mind. Finally the shelling stopped and the earth grew silent. A few moments later, he heard another nightingale answering in the distance.

After a long miserable winter, springtime in Italy came as a welcome reprieve. Surrounded by the filth and destruction of war, men longed to focus on something constructive. Spring's sense of renewal inspired a "back to the farm" movement on the beachhead.

Forcemen planted vegetable gardens right on the front line, watering and tending them daily. They set up small farms by purchasing animals from departing civilians, laying claim to abandoned livestock, or sneaking behind enemy lines to steal cattle and chickens from the Germans.

Ken and several of his men scoured their territory and collected a cow, six beehives, a flock of guinea hens, and a gaggle of goslings. They moved the menagerie with them from one outpost to the next, finding it a comfort to listen to the mooing and clucking in the evenings.

In one abandoned farmhouse, they found a cat with eight kittens and a rabbit with six baby bunnies. Upstairs a hen nested in an old armchair, a clutch of eggs beneath her.

Fresh eggs were a precious commodity in the Army, as much a currency as money. The men congratulated themselves on their find until Ken picked up an egg and heard cheeping inside. He gently placed it back in the nest. When the eggs hatched the next day, the soldiers carried the chicks downstairs and set them free. They watched quietly as the little balls of fluff swarmed away after their mother. Finally someone broke the silence saying, "Life goes on, doesn't it?"

The men's goslings were recently orphaned when found, so they couldn't be set free. At the stage when they were "all belly and feet and neck," their antics provided a lot of entertainment.

The goslings required protection from other soldiers, as rustling tended to be a problem among men grown tired of field rations. Ken herded the little geese into a box at night, but someone had to watch over the birds all day as "every visitor to our line casts wolfish glances at them." But according to Ken, "We all go armed, and are prepared for extreme measures to protect our geese if necessary."

Ken even risked admitting his veterinary background long enough to sex the young birds. "Our little goslings are four males and two females I think. They are just beginning to realize it themselves. Oh happy, happy goslings!"

In spite of the men's vigilance, one night someone made off with the birds. "We heard a noise and went out to investigate, half expecting a flock of Jerries. Whom ever it was got away with his booty. He was lucky not to get himself riddled."

The men's prized possession, a cow named Smokey, lasted longer than the goslings. Smokey gave about a quart of milk each day, and fresh milk was priceless. Another regiment kept a bull, and a lot of planning went into getting Smokey and the bull together at just the right time. The soldiers didn't expect to keep Smokey long enough to see her calf born – they just hoped to ensure their milk supply.

Because civilians had evacuated the towns around the beachhead, there was not a local economy at Anzio. There was no place to buy food, fresh or otherwise, and certainly no place to purchase souvenirs or gifts.

For Easter, which fell on April 9 in 1944, Ken had to improvise, so he made Mother a card. He gathered a few tiny wildflowers, small leaves, and thin blades of grass and fashioned them into a miniature bouquet. Using the Army's olive drab thread, he stitched the arrangement onto a piece of folded paper. Beside the bouquet he wrote "Happy Easter," and then he pressed it flat and mailed it.

Even as the men at Anzio busied themselves with pleasant endeavors, everyone on the beachhead felt anxious. They were all awaiting the coming invasion of Europe, hoping it would end the war and have them home by Christmas. Ken didn't think the First Special Service Force would be part of the big invasion, but "anything is possible." As it turned out, the Force went into action first.

# XI.
## ...as they turn from Praise.

In early May, General Frederick pulled the First Special Service Force off the front line at Anzio. New troops came in to relieve them, and Frederick's men went to the rear to rest and train, a sign that they would be facing combat soon.

Forcemen immediately stepped up their intelligence gathering. They needed to know what to expect when they launched their attack – how many Germans, their positions, and how well armed their enemy was. Every sector of the beachhead sent out patrols to find out what they would be facing.

Because the Germans had a clear view of Allied activity, men on the beachhead could move about undetected only after dark – no problem for night fighters like the FSSF.

On May 17, Ken set out on a harrowing reconnaissance patrol with three other officers. Shortly after ten p.m., the men climbed into a jeep and sped off into the darkness without benefit of headlights. They careened through the pitch-black night listening for the sound of oncoming traffic, swerving to avoid head-on collisions. The road was full of unseen holes, forcing them to hold on tightly to avoid flying out of their seats.

Eventually the jeep drew up in front of a half-ruined house. The four men got out and groped their way through a door hung with blankets. They stumbled down a set of steps leading to a musty cellar and found three men from another regiment crouched over a candle. Those men directed Ken's group to a rendezvous point farther down the road. The foursome set off on foot and soon found the patrol that would lead them to an outpost on the far edge of no-man's-land.

"We followed them across the fields, keeping to the ditches and walking carefully to avoid old mine fields on either side. Glowing red tracer shells arched into the sky. Gun flashes gave us light to see our way. At last we came to another house, and more men crouched round a candle in a crowded little room.

"We spent the remaining few hours of darkness in varying degrees of discomfort. My three companions crept into a narrow space under the floor. I was boosted up onto an old bed spring on top of a pile of sand bags. The spring sloped to one side and I was in continual danger of rolling off. Large shell holes in the walls let in a cold wind that my one blanket did little to stop. At 4:00 my teeth were chattering violently.

"Suddenly machine guns started chattering and bullets came cracking past the house. Mortar shells came whining down to crash in the field behind.

"It was just starting to get light, and it was necessary for us to get across to the barn to do our observing. The barn is only fifteen feet from the house, but in the daytime there is a German machine gunner who fires at anyone who ventures across. So we gathered behind the house, crossed our fingers, and made a dash for it.

"All about here there is a horrible smell of decaying cattle and dead Germans, but at this particular spot a long dead cow in the yard made an almost unbearable stench. Today, as the carcass heats up in the hot sunshine, it is getting worse than ever, and flies swarm in unbelievable numbers.

"This barn is quite the filthiest place I've seen yet. Literally knee deep in rubbish of every description. Flies swarm everywhere, and already the bugs have gotten under our shirts. We take turns climbing up on a table to look out under a broken tile. With field glasses we can see the German positions the details of which we came here to search out. It is hard to see much for the tall weeds and the bushes, but they are out there, watching us as we are watching them. We have to crawl past the window on hands and knees because if he sees us here he will start shelling. As a matter of fact, he has started already.

"About once a minute a shell whistles over the roof and lands in the field behind. Where will the next one go? Has he seen us? We can only wait and see. The last shell just landed about 30 yards from the house.

"I should be sorry to die now in this beautiful summer time, but accidents will happen."

Ken's reconnaissance party got the information they needed and made it back to camp just before dawn the following morning. They settled in to rest, knowing that soon they would need their strength.

May 23, 1944, dawned clear and sunny. At 6:30 in the morning, the Allies launched "Operation Buffalo," the breakout from Anzio and long push into Rome. A formidable force struck out from the right quadrant of the beachhead, with the FSSF's First Regiment spearheading their sector's attack.

Men of the 100th Infantry Battalion, the Japanese-American Nisei, covered the Force's right flank. Covering the left flank was Pollack Force, a provisional unit from the 3rd Infantry Division. Rounding out the attacking force were the Rangers' Cannon Platoon with 75mm cannons, the 645th Tank Destroyer Battalion, and two companies of the 191st Tank Battalion. Together they charged off the beachhead and into a field of ripening wheat.

By early afternoon the Force had accomplished its initial objective – cutting off Highway 7 to prevent the Germans from using it as an escape route from the south. But the FSSF advanced so far and so fast that they outran Pollack Force, leaving their left flank open and vulnerable when the Germans counterattacked.

Unprotected, Ken's Fifth Company came under intense fire, forcing them to withdraw and take cover in a shallow ditch that ran alongside the highway. Ken tried to talk the accompanying tank crews into pulling back with them, telling them that their light tanks were no match for the Germans' heavy armor. The tank men refused to turn back saying they had a job to do. Few survived the attack.

Fierce fighting continued throughout the afternoon and well into the night, but by morning the First Special Service Force and their accompanying units had broken the counterattack and claimed the highway. The exhausted men looked across the valley to their next objective, Monte Arrestino, a peak in the Lepini Mountains.

The Force took Monte Arrestino on May 25, the village of Rocca Massima two days later. From there they headed to Artena, a small town perched high atop a nearby mountain. Artena spills down the mountainside, its steep, narrow streets winding through neighborhoods of ancient stone houses. Its location gives the town a commanding view of Highway 6 running north into Rome, and made Artena invaluable to German troops using the road as an escape route. The Nazis fought hard to keep the town and the territory around it.

The Force moved into the Artena area on the afternoon of May 27 and immediately faced an unrelenting, twenty-four-hour barrage of German artillery. The following afternoon Third Division forces arrived, and the battle began in earnest.

"The fight didn't start till afternoon, but it went on all night and continued off and on for the next four days...was I tired...Funny thing was that I couldn't sleep even when there was an opportunity...It's no joke, having a whole company on your hands.

"We all got a bit jumpy towards the end, what with one thing and another. One time I was walking behind a bunch of men and happened to blow my nose. They all disappeared in a flash, some into holes, some flat on the ground. It was just like a conjuring trick. You see, I'd made a noise just like a certain kind of shell coming over. They couldn't seem to see the funny side of it at all.

"Funny things like that happen all the time. One dark night my runner and I were crossing a vineyard. The vines were strung in long rows, tied to wires. We were being shelled at the time, so we would run like mad between shells and flop to the ground before they landed. We kept getting tangled up in those damned vines and wires and often fell flat when it wasn't necessary. Pretty soon it got too 'hot' to move at all. They were bursting all around us. I heard my runner yell 'Come in here lieutenant!' so I wriggled over on my belly and found him in a little stone shed. I tried to squeeze in too, but the darn thing was full of firewood and I couldn't get my backside in at all. There was shrapnel flying all about and cold shivers running up and down my spine, but the situation was so damned ridiculous that we both started roaring with laughter and nearly smothered ourselves in the dust. What a night that was! Not all funny either. Not by a long shot.

"Another time we had been fighting all day and at last got into a great big ditch where we started to dig in for the night. There were some old Jerry dugouts there that were quite comfortable – after we had lugged out a few dead Jerries and shooed off most of the flies.

"One of our tanks came up from behind and wanted to cross the ditch. We showed him a bridge some distance off, but he couldn't be bothered and decided to go straight across. Well he teetered down into the midst of us and started up the other side, but it was too steep and he couldn't get out. Tanks attract artillery fire, you know, so we were expecting it to start pouring in at any moment. But there was that enormous machine, completely filling our ditch, roaring, smoking and churning the dirt like an angry dinosaur. You never saw anything so funny. We just stood around and roared and made fun of the tank men, who were swarming around like ants with a dead beetle. In the end they had to get another tank to pull it out."

The fighting around Artena was the most intense of the push to Rome, but the area finally fell to Allied forces. The FSSF moved out of Artena and through the neighboring town of Valmontone before liberating Colle Ferro on June 2. By the evening of June 3, Ken was in Colle del Finocchio, a little town on Highway 6 barely seven miles from Rome.

Thoroughly exhausted, Ken felt like a whole lifetime had been packed into the twelve days since he left Anzio. He had gotten only about an hour's sleep in any twenty-four. One day seemed to blur into the next. Some nights he was almost too exhausted to move, and on those nights, he told Mother, "I think of you and that gives me the strength to get out my little shovel and dig a little deeper into the ground before lying down to rest. That saved me more than once."

Without mentioning the more disturbing details, Ken referred to war as "a dirty business." He spoke freely of his feelings, however, saying that he had experienced something more akin to anxiety than fear. He admitted that he had been very worried about how he might react in combat – afraid he would be terrified, that he might panic. It was a relief when he found that his level of fear required less courage than he had anticipated.

Ken felt a sense of pride that he could stand the rigors of combat as well as most men and found he withstood it better than many. It surprised him to realize that during the fighting he barely noticed even the most dangerous and horrifying occurrences. Ken's solid sense of equanimity fared him well in combat, inspiring one of his men to remark, "By golly that Scotchman (sic) is a humdinger. He's as cool in a firefight as when he's out looking at flowers."

Ken led an entire company of men through thirteen days of combat even as he took another (leaderless) platoon through the roughest part of the battle. His actions inspired Ed Mueller to say that Ken was "a leader," admitting, "We must necessarily judge a man most of the time for his combat efficiency in a unit such as this. Because his job was combat, Ken performed this in a superlative, unspectacular manner. This is the opinion of those who knew and judged him."

At six o'clock on the morning of June 4, the First Special Service Force entered Rome, the first Allied troops into the city. There were still snipers holed up around town firing at soldiers and occasional skirmishes as men battled remnants of fleeing German forces. Local citizens poured out of their homes anyway, anxious to greet their liberators. Exuberant Romans packed the streets in welcome, hugging and kissing the soldiers, gifting them with flowers, bread, and wine.

By the end of that long day, units of the Force slowly began making their way to a rest camp in Tor Sapienza, a suburb of Rome. Exhausted after almost two weeks of combat, the men slept most of the next day. They gave little thought to anything other than food and rest until they awoke on June 6. The news that morning jolted even the most exhausted soldier wide awake. The Allies were in Normandy. It was D-Day at last.

# XII.

*I love thee with the passion put to use*
*In my old griefs,*

While Ken had been fighting his way to Rome, Mother had been on the move as well. In early May she had been transferred from Northington General Hospital in Tuscaloosa to Kennedy General Hospital in Memphis, Tennessee. The day she arrived at her new base, she received orders to ship out with the 141st General Hospital unit.

Mother had no idea where the Army was going to send her, but wherever it was, she assumed she would be there for the duration of the war. Censorship prohibited her telling friends and family that she was going overseas, but in a brief note to her parents she hinted in the vaguest of terms that she was preparing to ship out: She asked them to send along anything they thought an army nurse would find useful if she was to be away for an "extended period of time."

Her parents' understanding of what a nurse might need differed sharply from the reality of Mother's situation. In fact, few people understood what life was like for a woman in the military.

Although a small number of women had served in the previous war, in WWII there were branches of service comprised solely of women. Desperate to find volunteers to take over jobs and free men for combat, every branch of the armed forces launched propaganda campaigns to fill its ranks. Each one promised women opportunities to meet eligible bachelors, a chance to have the exciting social lives they missed after all the young men enlisted. Mother knew the propaganda was nonsense. Her naïve parents did not.

When the package from home arrived, Mother tore into it with great anticipation. She found that her mother had sent a beautiful evening gown, carefully layered among other equally frivolous and useless apparel that she had thought Mother would need.

The following day, still laughing at the idea of going off to war carrying an evening gown, Mother boarded an eastbound train. On the long ride, she dashed off letters to Ken, her parents, and to Mum letting them know that she had left Memphis. She couldn't tell them where she was going because she didn't know. No one on board knew.

The train pulled into New Jersey late on the night of June 5. As it slowed on approach to the station, Mother peered out the window, curious at the commotion on the platforms. There were throngs of people gathered there, all of them jumping up and down, screaming, and waving at the inbound passengers. The crowd seemed to be chanting something in unison, but no one on board could decipher their words. Finally, the train pulled to a stop and everyone heard clearly, "It's D-Day!"

It had been no secret that Allied forces planned to invade Europe; they had been amassing troops and weapons in England for over a year. There could be no final victory until the Allies landed on the continent, liberated the occupied countries, and fought their way into Germany. When and where the invasion would take place had been the big questions. As Mother's train rolled into the station in the middle of the night, it was already early on the morning of June 6 in Europe. The largest invasion force in history was converging on France's Normandy coast.

Mother's long train ride had taken her to Camp Kilmer, New Jersey, her last stop before shipping out. She spent just over a week there filling out the Army's endless paperwork and listening anxiously to news of the invasion.

Mother made friends easily and had quickly gotten to know the women she would be working with. In fact, a few of them were old friends from basic training at Camp Rucker. Granted a twelve-hour leave the day before they sailed, Mother and a group of her fellow nurses treated themselves to a memorable sendoff. They left Camp Kilmer for nearby New York City in the afternoon with plans to have dinner and see *Oklahoma!*, the new musical on Broadway.

The women had a picture taken as they relaxed before the show. The nurses, all proudly wearing their uniforms, are sitting at a table littered with dishes and tea pots. Most of the women are staring into the camera uncomfortably, but Mother appears to be enjoying herself. She is sitting at the far end of the table, one of two nurses smiling broadly. It is a professional photograph, a typical souvenir snapshot tucked into a red folder printed with the words:

*Billy Rose's Diamond Horseshoe*

*Paramount Hotel          New York City*

Mother, fifth from left, out with her friends.

The next morning, June 15, 1944, Mother boarded the USS *George Washington*, part of an enormous convoy. From the deck of the *George Washington*, she could see "…ships of all kinds, so many ships that I couldn't count them all. I never saw the beginning or the end of our convoy the whole way across the Atlantic."

In an attempt to avoid German submarines, the ships sailed a zigzag course bringing the crossing time to a full two weeks. As an additional security measure, the entire convoy had to observe a total blackout at night.

With plenty of time, little to do, and no light to do it by, Mother felt fortunate to have a variety of talent on her ship. The actor she had seen playing the part of Curly in *Oklahoma!* was aboard the *George Washington*, now just another soldier going to war. At night he sang on the darkened deck, and Mother thought he had the loveliest voice she had ever heard. She was sure that if the Germans heard him sing, they would spare the ship because his voice was so beautiful.

Mother arrived in Liverpool, England, exhausted from the strain of the dangerous crossing aboard the crowded troop ship. Because the future home of the 141st General Hospital still housed a men's division, medical personnel had nowhere to report. Their building wouldn't be available for days, and in the meantime, hospital staff needed housing. The Army sent most of the doctors and nurses to hotels and rooming houses in London.

Mother and her roommate, Bernice Stark, arrived in the city late at night, worn out from their travels. They found themselves billeted in a former rooming house taken over by the military. The two nurses dragged their belongings up one steep staircase after another to a room on the uppermost floor. They fell into bed exhausted, awakening a short while later to the sounds of a violent thunderstorm. Mother got up and closed the curtains to shut out the flashes of lightening that lit up the room, and the women slept like babies for the rest of the night.

Mother and Bernice (whom Mother always referred to as "Stark") awoke the next morning to a beautiful day. They dressed and joined other residents for breakfast, commenting on the terrible storm. The table fell silent as everyone turned to stare at the nurses.

The night before, while Mother and Stark slept, an air raid siren had sounded. Everyone in the building had evacuated to the nearest underground station, forgetting about the two new girls stuck away in their attic room. The weather had been fine. Mother had arrived in London for one of the last, and worst, German bombing assaults.

The Nazis had a new weapon, the deadly V1 missile. Twenty-five-foot-long bombs launched from catapults in northern France, V1s were programmed with only enough fuel to reach their targets. The missiles roared through the air until they ran out of gas and then fell silently from the sky. It was the sound of V1s exploding, not thunder, that had awakened Mother and Stark the night before.

Mother got a good laugh out of her close call, but she never again left herself vulnerable. The next time London's warning sirens sounded, she grabbed her pillow and blanket and got out of the building as fast as she could. Once in the city's darkened streets, she quickly melted into the throngs of people racing to the nearest air raid shelter, their way lit only by buildings already afire.

Eventually the Army processed the staff of the 141st to a military complex in southwest England. The massive installation, loosely referred to as "Le Marchant," lay on the outskirts of the town of Devizes. Charming and picturesque, Devizes nestles on a hilltop in Wiltshire county. It is an ancient market town built around the medieval castle at its center.

Numerous military installations dotted Wiltshire's vast Salisbury Plain. There was even a processing center for prisoners of war in tiny Devizes. The prisoners arrived at the train depot where guards lined them up, marched them to the center, and assigned them to one of the many POW camps located throughout Great Britain. Allied personnel divided the men into groups according to destination, then marched them back to the station to board trains bound for various camps.

Mother's welcome to Devizes was much warmer; her first impression was of a town overflowing with people. Her arrival coincided with the withdrawal of the American Fourth Armored Division, which was leaving to fight in France.

The unit had been in Devizes for some time, and many local women had married men in the division. The departing soldiers received quite a sendoff. Crowds lined the streets waving flags and crying as men marched past. Mother gaped in amazement at the sheer number of tanks moving out of Devizes in a line that stretched as far as she could see.

The men had vacated Le Marchant's Prince Maurice barracks. Their moving cleared the way for Mother's outfit to convert the building into the first of two general hospitals. The 141st opened in mid-July just as another unit, the 128th General Hospital, took over the newly vacated Waller Barracks next door. By mid-August, both hospitals had begun receiving patients as injured soldiers worked their way up the chain of evacuation from the battlefield.

A general hospital was the last stop for a seriously wounded soldier. He received initial treatment at mobile units – aid stations and field hospitals. Then he usually passed through an evacuation hospital before being sent on to a general hospital. Primarily reserved for patients needing long periods of recovery, therapy, or treatment, general hospitals usually occupied permanent quarters. They ministered to those whose wounds necessitated a more complex diagnosis.

The hospitals often had several specialists on staff: psychiatrists, urologists, neurologists, ophthalmologists, plastic surgeons, and thoracic surgeons. Orthopedic surgeons, however, bore the brunt of the caseload. There were enormous numbers of broken, shattered, and missing limbs.

When Mother wasn't on duty at the hospital, she lived in a one-story wooden barracks within Le Marchant. The Army sectioned off the building's interior to resemble rooms, affording nurses the illusion of privacy. In reality it was an unwelcoming place, cold and drafty, its plumbing inadequate.

Mother posed on an army jeep outside one of the many barracks at Le Marchant, Devizes, Wiltshire, 1944.

Regulations mandated that nurses place black-out boards over their windows at night. Mother and Stark thought the covers cast a depressing, institutional look over their quarters, so they made curtains to hide the dreary reminder that they might be bombed as they slept. Then Mother wrote Mum and asked her to send a dozen nails so that they could lend a bit of cheer to their space by hanging pictures.

While Mother was busying herself trying to make a barracks room in England look like home, Ken was settling into a new home in southern Italy sorting through his mail.

Ken and the men of the FSSF had awakened in Tor Sapienza on D-Day. The following day, June 7, they settled in for a long period of rest and relaxation at Lake Albano, about sixteen miles southeast of Rome. Although Ken's letters from Lake Albano couldn't tell Mother exactly where he was, he had referred to it as "yet another beautiful place" that he wanted to show her someday.

Set in Italy's picturesque wine-growing region, Lake Albano is magnificent, a crater lake with deep blue water and black volcanic beaches. In the shadow of Castelgondolfo, the Vatican summer palace, the men slept, swam, ventured into Rome, and listened anxiously to news of the fighting in France.

The Force spent three relaxing weeks at Lake Albano before sailing south to Salerno. From there they traveled forty miles down the coast to Santa Maria Castelabate. Ken wrote that he was in a lovely, peaceful place where apricots were ripe, camellias were blooming, and olive trees dotted the landscape.

Ken loved olive trees. He loved the way their leaves looked like embroidery when set against the sky. He sent Mother a sprig from an olive tree, knowing that she had never seen such a thing in North Carolina. He pointed out how dark the upper surface of the leaf is compared to its pale, silvery underside. The two colors were the reason the trees shimmered so beautifully in the sunlight, Ken told her, and why they appeared shot through with silver when the wind played over their branches.

It was on Italy's gorgeous southwest coast that the FSSF prepared for Operation Dragoon, the invasion of southern France. Once the Force established its headquarters at Castelabate, men began receiving mail regularly. The first letter Ken got came from Mother and its envelope bore an A.P.O. box number as the return address, meaning that she was no longer in the United States.

Army mail clerks in Italy had their hands full trying to keep up with so many troops on the move. Delivery had been sporadic since Ken left Anzio, and the few letters he had received prior to settling down in Castelabate had been backlogged mail – letters Mother had written months earlier, in March and April. She hadn't known that she would be shipping out when she wrote those letters, and even if she had she wouldn't have been allowed to mention it.

The letters Ken received in Castelabate had been written more recently. They carried her new return address, and the sight of the A.P.O. number filled Ken with dread. The return address offered no clue to her whereabouts. He had no idea whether she was in Europe or the Pacific.

Conscientious to a fault, Mother took army censorship to heart and her first letters offered little information. In subsequent letters, vague hints about the weather and what she did on her time off enabled Ken to place her in Europe. When he finally discerned she was in England, he rejoiced and immediately sent along the address of a friend in London.

Dr. May Smith, a professor, lived on Abbey Gardens, a lovely little street in Maida Vail. Dr. Smith was Ken's close friend, and he wanted the two women to get to know one another. He also wanted Mother to commit Dr. Smith's address to memory so they could use it as a rendezvous point some time in the future.

Ken tried to puzzle out Mother's exact location, but he never did figure out just where she was. He ascertained she wasn't in London, but thought she was most likely in Somerset or Devon, telling her, "It is pretty uncomfortable, not knowing where you are, or how you are making out, but I'm awfully proud of you. What tales we shall be able to tell each other some day!"

It drove Ken crazy to know that he and Mother were both in Europe and yet he couldn't get to her. In the continuing theme of "the Germans can't possibly hold out much longer," Ken made plans to search for her when the war ended and marry her immediately.

There was no more talk of a honeymoon in North Carolina or New Hampshire now that Mother was in England. There were so many things there that Ken wanted to show her, so many people he wanted her to meet. They made plans for the end of the war, for the honeymoon they would take in the British Isles. More than one of her letters closed with, "Don't forget to stop by and get me on the way home! I am waiting for you just as eagerly and anxiously as I used to wait for you at 408 Swift Avenue."

There was still a war to be won before Ken could come find Mother in England, however, and he had no choice but to continue the tiresome life of a combat soldier in Italy. He had grown increasingly weary of his lifestyle, saying that the hardest part was "being gone so long from home. Sometimes the longing to be home again becomes almost intolerable."

Ken yearned for "everything that is old and peaceful and clean, well loved and well cared for." Homesick for Mother, his family, and the cleanliness and comfort of 408 Swift Avenue, Ken waited anxiously for the end of the war, saying he just wanted to "come home, burn my uniform and forget the whole thing."

# XIII.
## *...and with my childhood's faith.*

Mother fell quickly into the rhythm of her new job and its shifts of twelve hours on, twelve hours off. She had no choice but to get in sync rapidly as fighting on the continent produced casualties at an astounding rate. Soldiers she had met on the Atlantic crossing only a few weeks earlier were already back with her, wounded now.

Seeing old friends and acquaintances renewed Mother's hope of a chance encounter with Ken. Although it was a big army in a big world, both Ken and Mother ran into old friends frequently. They knew that it was possible the two of them might cross paths someday. She never lost hope that they might happen upon each other, once telling Ken that "I passed by our Receiving Office today and saw a patient just coming in with a pipe in his mouth. For a moment I thought it was you and my heart came into my throat. My heart really stands still when I think that you and I may run into each other."

When Mother wasn't working her twelve-hour shift or catching up on sleep, she inspected her new surroundings. The beautiful Kennet and Avon Canal winds through Devizes, and the path that runs along the water's edge kindled memories of walks she and Ken used to take along the Eno.

She enjoyed her trips into Devizes – the local people treated visiting military personnel well. In fact, "the Lord Mayor himself" once invited Mother to a dance at the Town Hall.

The ballroom in Devizes is elegant, a showplace more befitting a palace than the administration building of a small rural village.

Compared to the endless sorrow in the hospital and the grim military surroundings at Le Marchant, the ballroom's glittering chandeliers and ornate musicians' balcony seemed to belong to another world.

Many townspeople attended these dances, and Mother made a few friends. Occasionally, someone invited her to their home.

Through the Army PX and packages from home, Mother often had access to items not available locally. She shared her good fortune with the friends she made in Devizes and usually took along a gift of food when she dined with a local family. She once surprised her favorite couple with a bag of popcorn, a coveted treat for Americans overseas. The couple was older and far too polite to tell her that they had never heard of popcorn. They accepted her gift graciously and thanked her profusely. On Mother's next visit, she asked if her friends had enjoyed her present. The couple looked at one another uncomfortably and admitted that they had not. "We boiled it for hours, but it never got soft enough to chew. How *do* you prepare it?"

The little booklet, "A Short Guide to Great Britain," given to all army personnel prior to arrival, had warned Mother to be sensitive should she be invited to eat with an English family. It had alerted her that the food set before her might be the family's entire week's rations, and she shouldn't overeat.

Expensive cuts of meat were among the first foods rationed when war began. By the time Mother arrived almost five years later, mutton was one of the few meats commonly available. Everyone ate it so often that friends occasionally greeted one another with a jocular "Baaaah!" rather than "Hello."

Although it was among the first meats rationed, pork could still be had in the Wiltshire countryside. Mother loved big English breakfasts with their "wiggly bacon."

Invitations to tea and Sunday night suppers were Mother's favorites even though they made her homesick for Mum and her old life in Durham. "Another Sunday in the E.T.O., Ken, and there is still that overwhelming nostalgia for tea at 408 Swift Avenue. As you have said so many times, it is memories like that that impel me to go on, but these same memories leave me desperately lonely in the meantime."

Mother had little time to dwell on her loneliness. She worked long hours at an exhausting, but incredibly rewarding, job. She loved her patients, always amazed at how grateful they were for the smallest kindness. Many soldiers came to love her too, a smiling Florence Nightingale with soft, cool hands. She regarded them as heroes even though at thirty-two she was a good bit older than most of them.

The average age of a soldier in World War II was twenty-six. The majority of Mother's patients were front line troops, however, and tended to be much younger, often only nineteen or twenty. Her age probably gave her something of a maternal aura for the younger men who, wounded and far from home, missed their own mothers desperately.

In a general hospital where patients routinely stayed for sixty days or more, patients and staff got to know each other well. With knowing Mother came knowing about her fiancé and she wrote Ken that, "There are lots of enlisted men over here who wish you well. They are my patients and ward men. Also lots of officers because I can't refrain from talking about you. Everyday some of them ask if I have heard anything."

Once, when she hadn't heard from Ken in a long while and concern was evident on her face, one of her patients tried to reassure her with a compliment. "Lieutenant, don't worry about him. If he was lucky enough to get you, then he is lucky enough to get through any war."

Mother, front row, left, with friends from the 141st General Hospital, Devizes, Wiltshire, 1944.

Mother's loving care formed a bond with patients, and they often wrote her after they left the hospital, sometimes sending her small gifts. She collected a number of trinkets: foreign currency, embroidered handkerchiefs, tiny painted wooden shoes from Holland, a medic's armband, the insignia from a Nazi uniform, a card from "T/Sgt. Quint Robertson" with its fabric insert embroidered *Greetings from France*, a myriad of unit patches, and small mementos.

Army nurses treated men who suffered from a variety of injuries. Mother's patients were blind men, amputees, and burn victims – usually tank men who escaped their burning vehicles or soldiers hit by incendiary bombs. She saw men who had been ripped apart by bullets and shell fragments, and men who had no visible scars, whose bodies were intact but whose minds had been shattered by war. She thought those were the saddest cases of all, and the psychiatric wards always seemed to be overflowing.

Mother, far right, wearing her nurse's cape, 1944.

An important part of Mother's job involved writing letters for patients who could no longer do so themselves, helping to prepare families for the homecoming of seriously wounded men. Her workload was endless, leaving little time to do more than work and sleep. Still, in spite of the long hours she spent at the hospital, Mother made time to write Ken almost daily. Her letters speak of how challenging her job is, but her words are always tempered by the knowledge that his situation is far more difficult.

"I know you are a tired man, wherever you are but still, dig in for me please. I shall always love you too much. I wish I could be there to stroke your brow and fill your pipe. Darling, be careful and hurry back to me. Every day seems like an eternity. I have seen so much and heard so much that is horrible. I dare not live more than one day at a time. I can only hope and wait and pray. These three things sustain me."

At least once a month, Mother sent Ken a box of things she thought he might need or enjoy. She usually included little luxuries in the parcels, things like his favorite pipe tobacco, Granger. He could never find any Granger, but Mother was happy to keep him supplied, grateful for the chance to inhale the tobacco's familiar aroma once again.

She often sent Ken books, and she always stuffed the boxes full of candy. Ken loved sweets, especially chocolate, which was at a premium during the war. Mother never cared much for chocolate and always sent her rations to him.

Each little crevice of the boxes held a special treat. Fragile articles arrived cushioned by bits of clean rags and steel wool that he could use later to clean his mess kit and polish his weapons. New handkerchiefs, a true luxury item, provided protection for precious foods, with bouillon cubes and tea included to disguise the taste of water purified with tablets.

Mother knitted socks for Ken and usually tried to tuck a pair or two in each of her packages. It always pleased him to find clean, dry socks as his feet were perpetually cold and wet. On a few occasions, she included a photo, and this pleased him even more.

Ken wrote long thank you letters for every box he received, often mentioning each item individually. Only once did he make a negative comment, and that concerned some small, yellow soaps Mum had sent him. They looked so much like caramel candy that he had eaten one and hadn't been able to get the taste of soap out of his mouth for days.

When Mother managed to find a bit of free time, she tried to tour as much as possible, anxious to see for herself the things that Ken had talked about over the years. Working the day shift gave her only one afternoon off each week, but the night shift sometimes offered an entire day free. She took advantage of every opportunity to explore her new home. Devizes is about ninety miles from London, close enough to take a train into the city. Mother went as often as possible, then came home and wrote Ken long letters reporting on everything she had seen.

A place she visited repeatedly was "The Old Curiosity Shop" on Portsmouth Street. A devoted reader of Charles Dickens, she purchased numerous volumes of his books in the tiny hardbound editions sold in the shop. She bought leather-bound copies when she could afford them and in all the books she wrote her name and the date on the flyleaf in her distinctive, pointed script.

Even with its bomb damage, London was an exciting place for a girl who had grown up on a farm in North Carolina. Mother spent hours wandering about, window shopping and browsing through the small stores that lined Bond Street. Although a few shop windows still managed to look "pre-war," inside there was little to buy.

Mother didn't let anything deter her or diminish her fascination with the city. She picked her way around the rubble from bombed out buildings and took in the tourist sights that remained open. She searched out places Ken had spoken of over the years, looked up Dr. Smith and several of Ken's old friends, met a few of his relatives, and visited schools he had attended. She went to Oxford, where Ken had spent the first twelve years of his life, and located places he once called home.

As a member of the armed forces, Mother could circumvent at least one difficulty facing travelers during the war. With food shortages so severe in England, the U.S. military established "messes" throughout London to feed its personnel, and Mother frequented an Officers' Mess in the city.

In typical military style, the Army transformed the gorgeous ballrooms of stately old hotels into utilitarian dining halls. Long lines of tables placed end to end ran the length of once elegantly appointed rooms. Along one wall stood a serving line with its stack of metal trays – the type with pressed indentions for food.

Officers could request as much food as they wanted from the enlisted men who doled out the meals, but they had to eat all they asked for. Wasting food was illegal in England, and the U.S. military enforced the law.

The Officers' Bar opened an hour before dinner. Everyone queued up early, hoping to get a drink from the one bottle of premium scotch or bourbon available. Beer flowed regularly during the war, and there was plenty of gin as well, but good scotch was difficult to come by, and bourbon was like gold. Once the one or two bottles of desirable spirits were depleted, choices were limited to beer, weak scotch, or the standard cocktail of those lean years, gin mixed with an orange drink called Squash.

If Mother didn't have the time or money to go into London, she explored closer to home. Le Marchant was not far from Devizes' town center, a distance covered easily by a short bicycle ride or a pleasant stroll through a beautiful park.

She went into town often, usually stopping at her favorite fish and chips shop to purchase greasy fried fish and potatoes, drenched in vinegar and wrapped in a newspaper cone. She strolled the path along the Kennett and Avon Canal or passed happy hours wandering about town. Hoary roofed structures dating from the 16th and 17th centuries line Devizes' narrow streets, mixing easily with buildings hundreds of years younger. Mother enjoyed milling about town, admiring the picturesque half-timbered houses, quaint stone churches, and charming cobblestone walks. She needed time away from the sadness and suffering at the hospital.

On pretty days, she liked to bicycle around Wiltshire. The countryside enchanted her, and she found the surrounding villages charming. The fact that Mother found the surrounding villages at all is amazing.

She had no sense of direction, and England had almost no road signs. All were removed early in the war when the threat of invasion was greatest. In the event German soldiers parachuted into the countryside, locals hoped that a lack of directional signs might disorient them, hastening their capture. Once Allied victory appeared certain and the threat of invasion remote, officials replaced the signs and made travel much easier.

Mother, right, and a friend setting off from Le Marchant on bicycles,
Devizes, Wiltshire, 1944.

Mother enjoyed exploring and thought the English bikes with their
three speeds quite luxurious. Her excursions brought back memories
of Sunday afternoons spent with Ken in Durham. After every outing,
she returned to her tiny barracks room and wrote him long letters

describing the most recent adventure in detail. She told him about the trees, flowers, and animals she had seen, gave him a weather update, and let him know how long she was gone.

Although she freely admitted that it was a poor substitute for his company, Mother shared her experiences with Ken by carrying his last letter along in her pocket. In fact, she always kept his latest letter with her, reading and rereading it as she went about her day. Back in her room, to Stark's amusement, Mother would spread the pages of Ken's letters out on her bed so that they were always in view. With the arrival of each new letter, the worn one went into her footlocker and the whole process began again.

# XIV.

*I love thee with a love I seemed to lose*
*With my lost saints,*

As Ken settled into the training routine in Castelabate in the summer of 1944, it was nearing a year since he had arrived overseas. He expected to have some leave time in October, although he was quick to say that nothing was ever certain in the Army. Now that Mother was in England, he hoped to meet her at Dr. Smith's London home. He and Mother exchanged frequent letters planning their rendezvous.

In spite of the arduous training, Ken enjoyed life on Italy's breathtaking southern coast. He spent every morning paddling around the beautiful blue waters of the Tyrrhenian Sea learning to use the rubber boats that would take the FSSF ashore on invasion night. The men learned to handle the small boats with precision and quickly mastered maneuvering the craft in formation. They also practiced scaling cliffs, another skill necessary for the coming invasion.

Forcemen took their training seriously, ever mindful of the recent carnage on some of the Normandy beaches. Troops would enter France from the south this time and sandwich the Germans between Allied lines. The FSSF, the American 3rd, 45th, and 36th Divisions, three Free French divisions, and a unit of French commandos known as Roméo Force were to mount the assault. While those forces invaded from the sea, the First Airborne Task Force, a unit formed from remnants of French, British, and American parachute troops, was to drop inland, blocking a German retreat from the coast.

Susan Lentz

The First Special Service Force had orders to seize and secure the Iles d'Hyeres – rocky, rugged islands located off France's southern coast about twenty-five miles east of Toulon. The FSSF was to precede the invasion force by five hours and knock out enemy artillery batteries that endangered landings on the mainland.

On August 11, the First Special Service Force left Italy and sailed for the island of Corsica. There they had two days to prepare for the invasion with free time to swim, fish, and relax in the sun. Ken thought Corsica was even more beautiful than the Italian coast they had just left, and he added the island to the growing list of destinations for his future travels with Mother.

At midday on August 14, the men of the FSSF left Corsica in a convoy of troop ships, cruisers, destroyers, and PT boats, along with the battleship HMS *Ramilles*. Ken had transferred out of Fifth Company at the beginning of August when the original Company Commander returned to the line. He was now a platoon leader in Third Company under the command of his old friend, Bill Merritt. Both men sailed towards the Cote d'Azur on the HMS *Prince Baudoin*.

Loaded down with equipment, Ken climbed down the ship's cargo net shortly before midnight carrying on him his knife, a Colt .45, a rifle, twenty pounds of ammunition, forty pounds of explosives, a detonating cap, four grenades, an entrenching tool, a canteen of water, and a box of K-rations. He dropped into a rubber boat loaded with Forcemen and silently paddled off into the darkness.

About 1:30 on the morning of August 15, Ken landed on the island of Port-Cros, coming ashore between Cap du Tuf and Port-Man. He and his platoon scurried across a narrow strip of beach and rappelled up the cliff side that loomed over the shore. Still undetected, they began making their way inland.

This was not Ken's first time on Port-Cros. He had visited the island nearly fourteen years earlier on a hiking trip with a friend named Fabergé. They had camped on the very beach the Force landed on but "this time the reception was less friendly."

Port-Cros proved to be a difficult island to invade. There were several fortifications on the coast, some dating back to Napoleon's days. The old forts were solid stone with walls so thick and well-built that they were impervious even to air bombings.

As Company Commander, Captain Bill Merritt led the attack on one seemingly impregnable fortress. Surrounded by a massive wall, the star-shaped Fort l'Estissac had only a single entrance. Bill led his assault platoon straight for the fort's iron gate, bursting it open with bazooka fire. The surprised Germans rallied quickly, raining grenades and gunfire onto the Forcemen. A vicious firefight ensued, but the Force pressed the attack and the Germans surrendered.

Fort l'Estissac no longer posed a danger to the invasion, but the cost had been high. Ken lost his friend Bill that night. As Bill lay mortally wounded, one of his men tended his commander's injuries and administered morphine to ease the pain. Then the soldier assigned a Canadian corporal named Gordon Baker to sit with Bill until the end. Baker sat on the cold ground in the darkness, cradling his captain's wounded head in his lap until a medic came along and told the young corporal that Bill was dead.

Over the next two days, Forcemen cleared Port Cros's other strong points of resistance and then moved onto the continent for some much needed rest. They spent the nights of August 17 through 19 at Sylvabelle, a missionary rest home on the French coast near Cavalaire. There the FSSF received orders to replace the British Red Devils within the First Airborne Task Force, the unit that had parachuted inland on invasion night.

On August 21, the FSSF met up with the First Airborne Task Force southwest of Grasse near the village of Le Planestel. Together they began moving up the coast, pursuing German troops retreating toward the Italian border.

As the FSSF worked its way from one village to the next, men combed the countryside looking for Germans. On one patrol, Ken's platoon spotted an old stone farmhouse that they suspected was being used as an enemy outpost. The men crawled toward the house on their bellies, finally getting close enough to see that a lone, very young German soldier sat guard at the front door. Ed Wolf, a sergeant in the platoon, carefully made his way over to Ken and told him that he could take out this one soldier easily.

3rd Co. 1st Regt. FSSF
A. P. O. 4994 etc.
20 Aug '44
Somewhere in France

Dearest Pearl,

Hold tight, here we come! It wasn't all together a pushover, but we made it and we're still pushing. You and I will make that rendez. vous yet.

Haven't had any mail lately and probably shellit for some time, but keep writing. That parcel you sent is still trying to catch up too.

Was lucky again and came off without a scratch.

Always your loving Ken

A letter Ken wrote from Sylvabelle on August 20, 1944.

"No," Ken replied, "I want to at least *try* to talk him into surrendering first."

When Ken called out to the young soldier in German demanding his surrender, the startled lad jumped up and ran inside. Immediately gunfire poured from the house, but in the fight that followed, Ken's platoon managed to take the outpost. When it was all over, the disgusted Forcemen found that only the officers were men; the others they had fought were just boys.

From Tanneron to Mougins, Valbonne, Plan de Grasse, Le-Colle-sur-Loup, St. Paul, and Cagnes-sur-Mer, Ken's platoon worked a circuitous course up the French Riviera. Ken found himself taking almost the same route he and Fabergé had hiked so many years before.

Although troops met with a good deal of fighting, the move northward had its pleasant moments. The FSSF liberated a number of towns along the way – Grasse, Villeneuve-Loubet, Vence, Drap, L'Escarene, and La Turbie. Ken wrote that they were welcomed everywhere "like conquering heroes, being fairly overwhelmed with kindness by the French people."

Celebrating villagers wept tears of joy and jammed the streets so tightly that soldiers had difficulty getting through. From every window hung French and American flags, many homemade, all carefully hidden from the Germans until that long-awaited day. Beneath the flags, ecstatic citizens surged toward their liberators. Forcemen met with bear hugs and kisses, "many of them garlic flavored...Bristly old men, beautiful young girls and all, they throw themselves upon us and kiss us on both cheeks."

Once Forcemen secured a town, they usually received a formal welcome from the mayor and high-ranking local officials. Citizens, including proud members of the local resistance, turned out in their best attire to honor the occasion.

Town officials greeted the highest ranking officer with a handshake and a kiss on each cheek, and then the mayor and the Allied commanding officer took turns addressing the cheering crowd. Afterwards, local bureaucrats feted the officers with wine and consulted them about any business at hand. Usually officials asked for help obtaining supplies or for permission to punish collaborators.

Meanwhile, in the streets, rejoicing townspeople gifted the Forcemen with hoarded treasures. Villagers loaded the soldiers' arms with fruit, vegetables, cognac, and an occasional "pathetically withered" chocolate bar saved since the earliest days of the war.

Ken especially welcomed gifts of fruit – grapes being a particular favorite. Having eaten his way through the vineyards of Italy, he was now enjoying those of France. He stopped his men every time they passed a vineyard and allowed them to rest for a few minutes while he gorged. When grapes weren't available, Ken was happy with most any fruit as a substitute saying that the figs, plums, and apples fairly melted in his mouth.

By the afternoon of August 27, the Force was in St. Laurant-du-Var where they rested for two days. Early on the thirtieth, they crossed the Var River. With the rest of First Regiment forces, Ken's platoon pushed southeast to St. Isadore and St. Sylvestre. By September 4 they were in Bausset and La Grave.

The FSSF established their rear headquarters in the city of Nice, and frontline troops moved east up the coast. Ken wrote Mother that it was "hard to find 10 minutes to write to you now. There is always time to think of you though, and I do so constantly."

With the liberation of Menton on September 7, the First Special Service Force had fought its last major battle. Less than a month after going ashore on the Hyeres Islands, the men of the Force had reached the end of the line in France. They settled in to hold their position in the Maritime Alps, the mountains along the French-Italian border.

While men in Force Headquarters were enjoying grand lodgings in fine homes and hotels on the Riviera, soldiers on the frontline were not so fortunate. Located somewhere near Castillon, inland from Menton, Ken was living on the side of a road in a hole dug under an abandoned concrete mixer.

Being in the mountains again was a thrill for Ken despite the difficulty of fighting in the rough terrain. He described his new location, writing that "We are in high, rocky mountains and I am enjoying it. Of course, Jerry sometimes makes it more exciting than we like, but he hasn't got his old punch anymore."

To hold their mountainous position, soldiers had to keep continuous pressure on German troops. Forcemen went out frequently under the cover of darkness to flush the enemy out of hiding or push them further back toward Italy.

Six of Ken's men from Third Company, First Regiment:
Left to right, Front row: Ed Wolf, Don Courtney, Cy Mermelstein;
Second row: Charles Kaifes, Steve Stefenson, Ed Helm.
Winter Palace Hotel, Menton, France, November 1944
*Photo courtesy of Cy Mermelstein.*

On September 14, Ken received orders to clear a unit of Germans from a nearby ridge. He gathered his platoon and briefed them about the upcoming patrol: its size, time of departure, objective, and plan of action. After the briefing, one of the men told Ken that he wasn't going on the patrol – *wouldn't go* on the patrol. He was sure that if he went out that night he would never return, certain that he would be killed. An argument ensued, but Ken had the last word: The soldier had to go. It was a combat patrol and they needed every man.

Early on the morning of September 15, the men blackened their faces with burnt cork and taped their dog tags together to silence their rattle. They set out from camp about 4:30, well before daybreak.

The terrain was treacherous, with enough brush to provide cover for both the Force and any furtive Germans. The line of soldiers started up the mountain on a switchback trail, the zigzag formation used to ascend steep slopes. They proceeded cautiously in the crouched posture so often associated with men in combat – bent slightly at the waist, head down.

Daylight began to break, providing enough light to discern a silhouette, though not quite enough to see clearly. The unit continued its trek upward, arriving at a particularly precipitous area where Ken gave the order to halt while he went ahead to scout the situation.

The order worked its way back to Ed Wolf who was near the end of the line, barely out of camp. Ed had just gotten the word to stop moving when the soldier next to him suddenly jumped up, shouted "German!" and fired his rifle. Ed looked up just in time to see Ken's helmet fly into the air.

Shot by one of his own men, Ken died instantly on that mountainside in France.

The shot that killed Ken gave away the patrol's position so the men aborted their mission and withdrew. A short while later, a party went out to retrieve Ken's body. The soldiers commandeered a farmer's donkey and hauled Ken back to camp.

That afternoon men who had been on the patrol were called into Headquarters for debriefing, a chance for the commanding officers to hear first-hand just what had happened.

Ed Wolf had plenty to say. He was particularly angry over Ken's death and railed at his superiors. Ed told them that they knew the man who shot Ken had a drinking problem, knew that he wasn't fit to be on the line. They should have done something about him.

Ken's staff sergeant, Clarence Bean, was even less objective. He wasn't so sure that it was an accident. The soldier who shot Ken was the same one who had refused to go on the patrol. Clarence had witnessed the confrontation between the two men the afternoon before, and it seemed to him too much of a coincidence that the soldier just happened to shoot the very officer he had argued with.

Clarence was well acquainted with the soldier who shot Ken. Both original members of the FSSF, they had trained together at Fort Harrison, Montana. Ken's staff sergeant had considered the soldier "a good man till right up towards the end. But he said he wasn't going on that patrol, and he didn't."

Cy Mermelstein, a private in the company, barely knew the man who shot Ken. Although new to the Force, Cy already realized that the soldier was troubled, describing him as "an edgy fellow, someone who shouldn't have been on the line because something was just *wrong* with him. Somebody said that he was shell-shocked from Anzio."

Corporal Maurice White had also heard that the soldier was shell-shocked, so shell-shocked that he had been taken off the line and hospitalized for treatment. Like Ed Wolf, Maurice was alongside the soldier in the long zigzag line up the mountain, but unlike Ed, he didn't know the man. Maurice had been in the company for almost three months, but he had never seen the man who killed Ken before the day of the fatal patrol. The soldier had only just rejoined the platoon.

Ernie Brown, a lieutenant in Third Company and the officer who led the patrol to recover Ken's body, saw the situation in a different light. Ernie hadn't been on the patrol, but an original Forceman himself, he knew the soldier who killed Ken. Ernie had spoken with the man shortly after the incident. The soldier told Ernie that he had heard someone moving through the brush and that he had given the order to halt. He claimed that he had called out the password not once but *three times*, and waited for the countersign. When no one answered, he thought it was enemy approaching and he fired.

One by one, men on the patrol testified to what they had witnessed, and the details of their accounts vary very little.

*Ken had ordered his men to stop and then gone forward a few yards alone. The instant he raised his head above the brush, a shot rang out. Ken was nowhere near the man who shot him – too far away to have heard any password. The bullet that killed Ken came from behind.*

But all the men agreed that it had happened in a split second, surely too fast for it to have been anything but an accident.

The man who killed Ken was taken away by MPs and supposedly discharged on a Section 8 – the Army's classification for those who are mentally unfit. But what happened after the fatal shot was fired bears little repeating because for Ken and Mother, it was over. All the promise that life held for the two of them was lost forever that September morning.

There would be no Ken to make that rendezvous in London or to find Mother in England after the war. There would be no honeymoon in the British Isles and no chance to visit all the beautiful places Ken had seen in the war.

There would be no Octobers spent in the mountains of North Carolina watching the leaves put on their brilliant show of color. There would be no leisurely Sunday mornings together at 408 Swift Avenue, and there would be no hikes on those Sunday afternoons. There would be no home with its library full of good books for their children to read and no little Janet or Mary McDougall to enjoy those books.

There would still be mountains and seas of course, but there would be no one to teach about such things and no one to learn what was under a dead log in the forest. There would be no kisses on the mouth at sunset and no kisses on the forehead at dawn. There would be no circle of happiness to be the envy of the world.

There would be nothing.

# XV.

*– I love thee with the breath,*
*Smiles, tears, of all my life!*

Nineteen days after Ken died, Mum got the tragic news. She immediately wrote to Mother, but word travels fast in a small, academic community like Durham. It was a condolence letter from Mother's friend Flo that arrived in England first. Mailed from North Carolina the same day as Mum's letter, in a cruel twist of fate Flo's note arrived two weeks earlier. Crushing news made all the worse because Flo assumed Mother already knew. Mother opened the envelope expecting a chatty letter full of gossip and tales of the latest happenings in Durham. Instead she read, "I am so very sorry to hear that Ken is dead."

Mother's world shattered when she read those heartbreaking words. She was devastated, inconsolable in her grief. And that is how Stark found her – devastated and inconsolable, but resigned to news she had feared was coming.

For some time Mother had been plagued by a feeling of uneasiness about Ken, a sense that had become stronger as August moved into September. Her stirrings of apprehension had taken on an air of foreboding after she had a disturbing dream.

"My dearest Ken darling, I had a dream this afternoon when I was half asleep and I thought that you were there beside me. You had your head resting on my arm and you were smoking your pipe. It was cruel to awaken completely and find you not there."

Mother wrote those words to Ken shortly after she awoke from a nap on September 18. Although she told him a little about her dream, she left out the more disturbing details. Her letter failed to mention that she had seen a bandage wrapped around his head or that he had spoken, telling her, "You are going to have to be strong and carry on. You shouldn't hate the man who did this. We had a lot in common. He liked to camp and hike. We could have been friends."

The dream had seemed disconcertingly real to Mother. She remembered that it was the smell of Ken's pipe that had awakened her. When she awoke completely, she felt in her heart that he was dead.

Still, Mother continued to write Ken almost daily in an effort to reassure herself that everything was fine, that it was only a dream. The letters written after his death are sweet and loving. They express concern about not hearing from him and wonder where he might be. "Belgium? Berlin?" Phrases from her letters seem almost prophetic. "Ken, just remember that I only love you more as time goes on…However long it takes, I will be waiting…I love you. Forever, too."

The letter Mum had written on October 4 telling Mother of Ken's death didn't reach England until October 24. Mother answered Mum the next day, the first letter she had been able to write to anyone. She wrote a letter of condolence, reaching out to comfort Mum. "These two weeks have been hard and my heart has bled for you. You have had more than your share of grief, Mum, but I know that you are not one to become bitter.

"Everyone who has known me here has felt that they have known Ken, too. And so when the news came it seemed to put a gloom over the entire hospital. Mum, I have been going on with my work, and work gives its rewards.

"I never thought that I could live, or want to live if anything ever happened to Ken. However, Ken has seemed so near me these past few weeks that I have found an inner strength that I did not know I possessed. I dare not become bitter for fear of losing this feeling of nearness to him."

Mother goes on to refer to *our* grief and to inquire how Lesley and Angus are bearing up, sending them her love. In the end, that is how she always coped with life's difficulties – by looking beyond herself.

At the time she wrote to Mum, neither woman knew how Ken died. The telegram Mum received from the War Department stated only that he was killed in action on September 15. But Mother didn't believe that Ken had been killed in combat – she was sure that he had died in some sort of accident. Unable to envision any other explanation, she told Mum, "I still feel that he fell in an avalanche." Mother looked to Ken's commanding officer for answers and wrote him asking for details about Ken's death.

It was Major Ed Mueller, Ken's friend from the Mountain Warfare School, who replied to her inquiry. Ed worded his letter carefully, skirting the real circumstances surrounding Ken's death. "One night he was reconnoitering the terrain in front of us. He and a small group of his men were well over a mile in front of our front positions. It was precipitous mountain country with a large amount of cover (trees and brush). At a point which seemed suspicious he halted his group and proceeded forward alone. A moment later he was shot in the head – killed instantly."

Ken's old friend left out the more painful details, but told no lies. In an effort to spare Mother a lifetime of anguish over the needlessness of Ken's death, Ed performed a kind and well-intentioned act. The natural assumption was that a German had fired the fatal shot, that Ken had died in combat.

Mother kept the letter from Major Mueller, but she kept only a few other condolence letters. They all echo the same theme. "If I had a son, I should want him to be just like Kenneth, for he was 'one of Nature's Noblemen,' " "…he was to me the most ideal expression of the flower of our race that I have ever known," "…this, the greatest of all tragedies has affected me deeply. It is scarcely believable that Ken, a man of such magnificent physique and such tremendous strength of character should suddenly pass from amongst us without the slightest warning."

His death must have seemed even more inconceivable to Mother. Ken was both her past and her future.

# XVI.
## ...and, if God choose,

Mother had no choice but to tackle her future alone. Outwardly at least, life went on. As the war dragged through the fall of 1944, changes began to take place in Devizes. In September, the POW processing center started retaining prisoners rather than moving them to various camps. The number of prisoners housed in Devizes grew rapidly until there was a full-fledged POW camp, Camp 23, at Le Marchant. With the added burden of so many prisoners, Mother kept busy, her work difficult, her hours long. Staying busy helped to distract her from her grief as she waited for Germany to surrender – something everyone expected to happen at any moment.

Where there are prisoners, there will inevitably be escapees. For a period of several weeks in the fall of 1944, Camp 23 experienced a rash of escape attempts. Some prisoners, unable to find a way out of England, grew tired and hungry and decided to turn themselves in. Others were captured by civilians or military, and still others were probably only pretending to escape. Those prisoners were most likely on reconnaissance missions and had no intention of actually getting away. They gave up or sneaked back into camp in order to report their findings.

Regardless of the reason, the Germans found themselves back in prison. British authorities generously allowed novice American intelligence officers to practice their interrogation skills on the former escapees. That turned out to be a stroke of luck for personnel at Le Marchant who learned of a much larger escape plan in the works.

Officials found that prisoners were planning a break-out, a massive escape said to involve the entire camp population. A few people thought that the plot was simply a routine escape attempt, but most people familiar with the situation believed it was much more.

One theory held that the escaped prisoners planned to make their way to the coast where German ships would be waiting to take them home to rejoin the war. Others familiar with the plot theorized that Hitler was too preoccupied to spare forces for a prisoner rescue. To supporters of that theory, the prisoners' escape was to culminate in an invasion from within, an attack on London.

The German prisoner Allied officials relied on for most of their information was notoriously unreliable, a consummate liar eager to trip up his interrogators and throw them off the trail of his own escape plan. Still, no intelligence could be ignored, certainly none that indicated so serious a plot in the works. Officers in command of Le Marchant believed that the prisoners planned to overpower their guards and seize all transportation and weapons in the camp, barracks, and hospitals. Soldiers from panzer divisions were to commandeer tanks while men from Luftwaffe divisions made their way to the nearest airfield.

Because it housed 7,500 prisoners, a breakout from Camp 23 alone would have been of major significance. But there were over a quarter of a million prisoners of war in Great Britain, dispersed into a number of camps spread throughout the countryside. Supposedly the escapees planned to increase their ranks by liberating 75,000 of their comrades along the way. While it is unlikely that the POWs could have overrun London, they could have left a wide path of death and devastation in their wake.

Originally the prisoners planned their escape for Christmas Eve, assuming the staff would be celebrating the holiday and could be caught off guard. Once aware of the plot, Allied personnel monitored the situation closely. When they got word that the escape had been moved up to December 16, they squelched the plan immediately, removing the instigators on December 14. They shipped the hard-core Nazis to secure camps in remote parts of Scotland to separate them from the regular German prisoners.

Mother always believed that the prisoners planned to attack London, although she didn't focus much on that aspect. The initial breakout concerned her more. She truly believed that she wouldn't have lived to see Christmas Day had the prisoners' intentions not been uncovered. She remained convinced that "They planned to kill us all!"

Actually, according to some of the POWs questioned later, personnel at the general hospitals weren't to be harmed. They were to become prisoners kept at the ready to administer aid to any Germans wounded in the rampage.

Mother never accepted that explanation. She understood that the escape was masterminded by the vicious Waffen SS, the true Nazis. They would have had few qualms about slaughtering anyone who got in their way, including hospital staff that came to the defense of their cohorts or patients. If Mother's horror over her possible demise was not completely well-founded, it was not far-fetched.

About the time the excitement in Devizes died down, things heated up on the continent. The Allies were continuing their drive toward Berlin when a surprise attack on December 16 stopped their progress in Belgium. Hitler's troops broke through Allied lines in a final attempt to stave off an invasion of Germany and turn the tide of the war.

Known as the Battle of the Bulge, this was the largest land battle involving United States forces. Occurring in and around Belgium's Ardennes Forest, it lasted from mid-December 1944 to the last week of January 1945. Victory in the Ardennes cost Americans dearly: 81,000 casualties with 19,000 of those being fatalities. Staff at the 141st and the 128th General Hospitals in Devizes geared up to admit vast numbers of critically injured men arriving from the Belgian front.

As hospital personnel struggled to recover from the shock of the planned escape and to cope with mounting casualties from the Ardennes, Christmas drew near. Mother noticed some of the prisoners decorating Camp 23 with three-dimensional, multi-pointed Moravian stars. A Christian denomination with deep German roots, the Moravian church has a large following in North Carolina. Mother always attended Christmas Eve services with her Moravian cousins, so the stars were a symbolic and meaningful part of the holiday for her. When she saw her prisoner patients constructing them out of old newspapers – the only paper they had – it touched her heart.

Mother found that most German soldiers were "as nice as could be," kind men and young boys caught up in the horror of war. Others glared at her with hate-filled eyes even as she ministered to them.

Although the care of prisoners was always secondary to that of our own troops, Mother tried to meet their needs even if they didn't appreciate her efforts at the time. Propaganda flourished in Camp 23, and a common rumor circulated that prisoners taken to the hospital often didn't return, that hospital workers killed them as they lay helpless.

One very young German patient to whom Mother was supposed to give an IV had heard these tales and assumed that the IV bag she carried to his bedside contained a lethal dose of drugs. The frightened boy fought valiantly for his life. No matter how Mother tried to explain, in a language he probably didn't understand, she couldn't abate his fears. He fought, kicked, hit, bit, and dodged her until she had to call for a ward man to help her get the boy out from under his bed. She gave the terrified lad his IV, and he recovered – much to his own surprise.

Mother may not have had a warm place in her heart for every enemy soldier, but she did her job professionally and assumed her counterparts in Germany did the same. When the Allies began liberating POW camps full of Americans and she saw the frightful condition of "our boys," she couldn't believe her eyes.

Once Allied forces liberated a camp, they processed former prisoners through a medical facility where a military doctor examined them. Almost all POWs were malnourished, but if they were otherwise in good health they went to a large holding center. The Army transformed warehouses, auditoriums, and most any building with a large open area into centers where former POWs could be cared for under observation.

The men usually needed delousing, and then they had access to hot showers, clean clothing and beds, healthy meals, and massive doses of vitamins. The military provided physical therapy as well as psychiatric counseling, and the former prisoners got liberal amounts of leave time.

A great number of POWs were in no condition to enjoy their newfound freedom. Many were near starvation, too sick to go into the holding centers. Those were the men Mother saw, soldiers who had to stay in the hospital until they grew strong enough to tolerate the long trip home. By mid-1944, the military had begun using air evacuation for some of the wounded, but most soldiers sailed home on troop ships. Either way was an arduous trip and many men were too weak to undertake the journey.

Army doctors, virtually all of whom were men in that time and place, diagnosed and determined the course of treatment for the former POWs. Then, at least at the 141st General Hospital, men had to step aside. The day-to-day care of former prisoners of war fell under the auspices of women; men weren't allowed near them unnecessarily. If a job was too big or too heavy for a woman or two, nurses called upon ward men. If there was a medical situation beyond the nurses' capability, they called for a doctor. Otherwise, the former prisoners who had been so traumatized by men lived in a world of gentle, soft-spoken women.

With scores of wounded still arriving from the Belgian front, the huge number of POWs at Camp 23, and American prisoners of war beginning to trickle in from newly liberated camps, Mother spent a busy winter in Devizes.

By mid-April, her workload began to drop off considerably. As the war wound down, there were fewer large battles and consequently far fewer casualties. General hospital personnel throughout England saw their patient numbers decline steadily as they sent men back to the lines or shipped them home, and no one came in to fill the beds. It was obvious that the end of the war was near. Hospitals began to consolidate their patient loads, merging some units in order to close others.

Eventually Germany could not keep up the pretense of a possible victory. Hitler committed suicide on April 30, 1945, and hundreds of thousands of German soldiers began turning themselves in to Allied personnel.

The Nazis agreed to surrender on May 7. Declaring the next day VE Day – for victory in Europe – people began to celebrate what Mother and Ken had waited for, counted on, for so many years. Most army hospitals held robust celebrations as their pharmacies contained good stocks of liquor. Once doled out to patients through prescriptions that read *Spirits Fermenti*, the "medicine" now served to celebrate the end of World War II in Europe.

Ken's death overshadowed most of the joy Mother felt at seeing the war come to an end. She celebrated with her friends and cohorts, but there was a void within her that parties and victory parades could never fill. One way she chose to commemorate the war's end was by going to church. The service she attended at Bath Abbey entitled *Thanksgiving and Dedication for Victory in Europe* was a series of hymns, prayers, and oral recitations in observance of the many sacrifices that had been made to win the long war.

Amid the celebrations on VE Day, Mother went to her commanding officer and requested a week's leave. With all the festivities marking the end of the war, she felt it would be easier to be away from Devizes with its memories and comforting to be with someone who also felt her deep loss.

Less than forty-eight hours later, she and two friends boarded a train for Scotland, the place Ken had loved above all others. They went to visit Ken's close friend George, a man Mother had known in the United States. The two of them corresponded frequently, with Mother often acting as advisor in George's love life.

Devastated by Ken's death, George had written Mother as soon as he heard the news, begging her to come spend time with his family in Scotland. She couldn't get away then; there were men to nurse and her need to keep busy was too great. But now she went to see George, and he showed her all the places that had once meant so much to Ken.

Mother and her friends had pictures made at a photographer's studio in Edinburgh, near George's home in Dundee. It was the sort of studio frequented by service personnel in those days, a place to have professional shots made in dress uniform. She posed for the standard portrait-type photograph in which she looks very professional, and the three women had a group photo made. Mother had a third picture made too, and in it she appears to be almost bursting with happiness. In that photograph, she is all decked out in the tartan of clan McDougall.

Ken and Mother had made countless plans for what they would do when the war ended, but when the time finally came, she had to face it alone. She left Scotland for Devizes in mid-May and began preparations to return stateside. Before she left England, however, she had something very important to do.

Mother took the trip she and Ken had planned to take as their honeymoon, an abbreviated tour of the British Isles. She and a few friends bicycled through the countryside of England and Wales. It wasn't the same trip she would have taken with Ken, meeting the people and seeing the sights he loved, but it was as close as she could come.

On June 15, 1945, exactly one year from the day she boarded the ship that brought her to England, Mother boarded the HMS *Queen*

Mother wearing the tartan of clan McDougall, Edinburgh, Scotland, May
15, 1945. This was her favorite photograph, framed and always on
display in our home.

*Elizabeth* for the trip home. She had orders to report to the Pacific front, so she expected only a few weeks' leave in the United States. When the ship docked at the end of June, she was once again at Camp Kilmer, New Jersey. From there she caught a train to Fort Bragg, North Carolina, the camp where she and Mum had visited Ken three years before. She spent a few days at Fort Bragg and then began a month's leave visiting her family in Winston-Salem and Mum in Durham.

Mother returned to Fort Bragg on August 7, believing she would soon be leaving for the Pacific. When she got to camp, however, it was abuzz with talk about something called an atomic bomb. No one had ever heard of the powerful bomb or knew what to expect. The new weapon brought about the surrender of Japan, and on August 15, 1945 – VJ Day – the world celebrated the end of the war. Grateful to have been spared the horrors of the Pacific theater, Mother settled in at her new assignment, Oliver General Hospital in Augusta, Georgia.

Before the Army took over, Oliver General Hospital had been the Forest Ricker Hotel. Elegant and refined in its day, the beautiful three story structure featured graceful arched windows on its uppermost floor. The hotel consisted of three wings: the building that fronts the street, with an additional building set perpendicular on either side. This resulted in a courtyard in back, a place for patients to sit in the sun and read or chat.

The Army used the hotel as the main hospital, increasing the space by building barracks to use as wards. Mother once again found herself among German prisoners of war who cooked and served most of the food at Oliver General.

A huge hospital, Oliver treated a variety of injuries. Once their wounds healed, patients faced months of rehabilitation there. Men had to relearn how to use injured arms, legs, and hands, or learn how to maneuver without them. As time passed, rehabilitation became the hospital's primary concern, and former soldiers made good use of the golf course that had once been part of the hotel.

Mother went to Augusta with a group of ten nurses, all recently arrived on the *Queen Elizabeth*. Like her, every nurse had at least a year's experience on the European front. Although she went to Augusta with friends, Mother arrived there with little baggage. In the confusion surrounding the war's end and the Army's endless red tape, someone didn't get word in time and her footlocker made the long trip to the Pacific and back without her.

This was of little concern to Mother. The footlocker contained only army-issued items anyway: uniforms, nurse's caps, army caps, her heavy overcoat, her navy blue nurse's cape with its red lining, a bedroll, and blankets. The important things, Ken's things, were with her always.

# XVII.
## *I shall but love thee better after death.*

Mother remained in Augusta until she finished her tour of duty on January 21, 1946. Then she returned to her parents' home in North Carolina where she found quite a crowd gathering.

After the war, people went to great lengths to locate old friends. Often contacting someone in person was the only way to know for sure who made it back. There was a lot of catching up to do as people tried to restore a sense of order to their lives and begin making plans for the future.

Mother had not only old friends looking for her, but suitors as well. They came to Winston-Salem in droves bearing gifts and proposals of marriage, pleading with my grandmother to intercede on their behalf. One of those suitors was a handsome army captain known by the nickname Prexy.

Prexy and Mother had met in Devizes. He had known her when she was engaged and was there when she learned of Ken's death. He must have admired the way she carried on after being dealt such a blow, and he must have cared a great deal about her because he gave her a very special gift.

The gift Prexy brought Mother was a large wooden box sixteen inches wide, nineteen inches long, and about three inches deep. It looks like a massive book with its top, bottom, and spine stained dark brown. Between the book covers, the other three sides are painted to look like the edges of paper.

The top of the box, which appears to be the book's front cover, bears the words "Treasure Chest" printed in large gold letters and positioned as if it were the title. Below the words are two small oval paintings: one of a young Mother in her army uniform, and one of Prexy in his. To the side of each picture, penned in gold paint, there is a handwritten account of the places where each of them served. The rest of the front contains various army insignia representing each of their units and large golden letters that say "Memoirs" and "ETO," a reference to the European Theater of Operations.

The cover has hinges and opens to reveal two wooden trays stacked one on top of the other and divided into compartments like those in a jewelry box. Under the trays there is a false bottom, for the men who crafted the box had lived through years of war and knew the value of a secret hiding place. In that hidden space rests a patriotic Christmas card mapping the Allied drive to Berlin and bearing the proud signatures of the craftsmen in Antwerp, Belgium, who contributed to the making of this cherished memento.

This is the box that provided so many hours of pleasure for my sisters and me as we were growing up, the box that held everything most precious to our mother. In it she kept souvenirs from her years with the Army Nurse Corps, and alongside them, her gifts from Ken.

I remember asking Mother about Prexy once – if she loved him and if he loved her – but I got only a faraway look and a vague, noncommittal response. There were many men who cared about Mother in the years after Ken's death, men who wanted to take his place in her heart. They were probably all fine men, they just weren't Ken.

Mother wasn't the sort of person to spend her life alone though. Eventually she chose to marry one of her many suitors. She and Alton Patterson had known each other before the war, when he had been her patient at Duke Hospital. Alton fell in love with her then, but she was dating Ken at the time and had no interest in other men. After the war he joined the long line of men looking her up, and to everyone's surprise, she married him.

They wed in Duke University's beautiful chapel on an icy December evening in 1946. Mother was a gorgeous bride dressed in her mother's handmade wedding gown. The dress is elegant in its simplicity: a cotton batiste gown made for my grandmother by her aunts shortly after the turn of the century. As the gown was hand carried from one aunt's house to the next, each woman contributed her specialty – tiny tucks, lace insets, perfectly matched sleeves. Three of Mother's sisters had already married in the gown; her fourth sister would wear it the next year. Some thirty years later, Anne and I would choose to wear it.

Mother married a Mississippi farm boy, eight years older and divorced to boot, a scandalous thing in 1946. Alton had been married to a woman named Mae who my aunt once described as "incredibly beautiful, but the meanest woman on earth." She may have been right. One day Alton came home from work to find his wife and his boss in compromising circumstances. He walked out of his house and out of his job and later granted Mae a divorce on the grounds of "desertion." This was a noble and gracious act in a time when chivalrous men took the blame for a divorce, no matter the real circumstances.

My father had not gone to war. Older, and beginning to show signs of the health problems that would take his life by age sixty, he made an important contribution to the war effort nonetheless – he was a pilot. He flew in an era when any level pasture was a runway, when flyers wore goggles, a tight leather helmet, and a bulky leather jacket for protection against the cold in the open cockpit. When he proved too old to enlist, he became a flight instructor and taught younger men to fly for the military.

These men were not his first students. Years earlier he had taught his stepson John to fly. A child as beloved by my father as if he were his own son, John was the reason my father stayed with Mae as long as he did. He and Mae were married for over ten years, from the time John was a child until he became a young man. There was a war raging when John came of age, so he joined the Army Air Corps, the predecessor of today's Air Force. He went to fight in the European theater, only to be shot down over Italy in February of 1944.

John's death came as a crushing blow to my father. Not only did he lose someone he loved dearly, but he blamed himself to some degree for having taught the boy to fly.

It is only speculation of course, but I have to think that this devastating loss was one of the reasons my father was so generous to my mother in allowing Ken's memory to be a part of her life.

I also suspect that my father felt a debt of gratitude to Mum. Mother had moved back to 408 Swift Avenue after the war and was still living with Mum when she and my father married. Many of Mother's friends and family were against the marriage. They found Mother's other suitors more desirable – younger men who had never been married. Mum must have supported Mother in her choice though, because if she had voiced any disapproval of my father, Mother would never have married him.

There was another reason behind my father's generosity, and of this one I am certain: He absolutely adored my mother. The competition for Mother's hand was intense, and he felt incredibly fortunate to be the one she chose. In a letter written shortly before their marriage, his unrestrained joy all but leaps off the page as he tells her that he has been in love with her since he was her patient.

My father went into marriage well aware that he was Mother's second choice, but she never made him feel that way. She talked with my sisters and me about what her life would have been like with Ken, but she never made any unfavorable comparisons between that life and her life with our father, and she never allowed any on our part. I know that she loved my father, and had it not been for Ken he might have been the love of her life. Regardless, she was a devoted partner.

Although Ken's gifts were Mother's most cherished possessions, after her marriage she never wore any of the jewelry he had given her. When my sisters and I grew up she encouraged us to wear some pieces, but she was a loyal wife and later, a loyal widow.

As she had done with the McDougalls, Mother truly made my father's family her own. My parents were married for nineteen years but my father suffered from ill health almost from the beginning. She took care of him through all the ups and downs, supporting the family when he no longer could. She was only fifty-three when he died and left her with three daughters to raise.

Mother worked until she was in her seventies as a matter of economics. It was a job she loved though, employed by the same doctor, Ross Love, for almost thirty years.

In 1972, for Mother's sixtieth birthday, Dr. Love and his wife gave her a trip to Europe. This was at a time when such a trip was a once-in-a-lifetime event, meant only for people of means. The tours were whirlwinds of activity, often covering ten or more cities in three weeks.

Thrilled at the prospect of her trip, Mother couldn't wait to see Europe when it was not at war. In early September, she and her friend Connie Taylor set off for New York to catch their Pan Am flight to London. It was the first time Mother had been back to New York since she stepped off the hospital ship HMS *Queen Elizabeth* in 1945.

Her itinerary covered the usual places: London, Amsterdam, Brussels, Lucerne, Munich, Rome, Florence, Paris, Madrid, and finally, Lisbon, before flying home. Mother followed along with the tour as far as Madrid. It was there that by prearrangement she left Connie and the group and made a side trip to the south of France.

On September 20, Mother, who spoke not one word of French, set off alone. She flew to Nice and then traveled to the little town of Draguignan. She arrived on a bus and got further directions from the friendly driver who spoke only French. She got off at her appointed stop, and as she walked away, the bus started off only to stop almost immediately. Windows popped open and passengers leaned out shouting words she didn't understand and gesturing for her to go in the opposite direction. Mother corrected her course, smiled, and waved them off.

It was a beautiful day. A typical fall day on the coast of southern France; the weather was warm and sunny, the sky clear and blue. Draguignan is only sixteen miles from the Mediterranean, close enough for balmy ocean breezes to give the town an exotic, tropical feel.

Mother set off down the street, walking a short distance before turning right at the first corner. After crossing a wide, tree-lined boulevard, she turned again and followed along a side street until she came to a black iron fence whose massive gates stood open on either side of a wide drive. She stepped through the gates and then stopped for a moment to look around.

A small stone house sat just to her right. Mother went inside, dropped off her suitcase, signed the guestbook, and found a man who spoke English to help her with directions.

Then she left the little house, skirting the walkway to cut diagonally across the manicured lawn. Mother had gone only a few yards when she found what she was looking for: Plot 3, Row 5, and the white marble cross that read:

# KENNETH D. MC DOUGALL
## 2 LT 1 SP SV FORCE
## NORTH CAROLINA    SEPT 15 1944

∞∞

Ken rests in a beautiful place. Rhone American Military Cemetery has a peaceful, intimate feel that makes it seem much smaller than the twelve acres it occupies.

A wide double walkway runs the length of the grounds, bisected midway by a fountain rising from an oval pool. There is a tiny open-air chapel built into the hillside at the back of the cemetery. Behind the chapel the hill is covered in oleanders, cypress, and the olive trees that Ken loved so much. More olive trees grow throughout the grounds.

Ken is one of 861 soldiers buried at Rhone. Bill Merritt is another. They lie not far from each other, the two old friends from Colorado, forever two young men in southern France.

I don't know how much time Mother spent at the cemetery, but I know that she stayed far longer than she had planned. She had come a long way to be with Ken that one last time and couldn't tear herself away to catch the last bus back to Nice.

The man in charge of the cemetery came to her rescue and hired a car for the return trip. The driver spoke only a little English, but he was a kindly, older man who didn't need words to comprehend the situation. A woman her age, all alone, visiting an American World War II cemetery needed no explanation for someone who had lived in France during the war. On the way to Nice he treated her to dinner, and when they reached the hotel he refused to accept any payment for the trip.

Mother and this Frenchman had had a wonderful time together and had found a great deal to talk about. Using sign language and his halting English, they had reminisced and shared stories about the war. There had been no language barrier. Mother had understood that he was thanking her. That, like her, he *remembered*.

# Epilogue

Mother lived another twenty-seven years after her pilgrimage to Ken's grave. She died without anyone ever telling her what had really happened to him, but she always felt that something wasn't quite right about the explanation she got from Ed Mueller.

After the war, several of Ken's friends from the First Special Service Force sought out Mother to meet her and pay their respects. The story she heard from them varied not at all from Ed's version of events. They too wanted to spare her any more pain. So in the years that followed she told this same story – that Ken died in combat, shot by a German.

Four years after Mother's death, I learned the truth.

My first conversation with a member of the Force was with Colonel Robert Moore, the man who commanded most of the night patrols at Anzio. He recalled Ken vividly, "How smart he was! What a quick study. I wanted him in my regiment desperately." He remembered a big man who smoked a big pipe, and like everyone else, he remembered Ken as a gentleman, a gentle man.

When Colonel Moore spoke of Ken's death as "tragic," I realized that he might be able to tell me something more about that terrible day. I asked him for any details he could recall.

"First," he said, "let me ask if you know how Ken died."

Thinking Major Mueller's version was an accurate account, I replied, "Oh yes, I know all about it. Ed Mueller wrote my mother and told her everything."

Colonel Moore expressed some surprise at my statement, but proceeded to tell me the facts as he remembered them. His version of the story didn't sound familiar though; he kept using the word "accident." At first I was sure that he had confused Ken with someone else. Soon it became apparent that he had not. Once I realized that the Colonel was talking about Ken, I asked if he had been killed by one of his own men, a victim of "friendly fire."

There was a pause that seemed to go on forever, and then Colonel Moore said very softly, "I'm sorry. I thought you said that you knew."

His words stunned me, and then left me numb as I realized that the truth was much more in keeping with the things Mother remembered Ken saying in her dream. "You mustn't hate the man who did this. We had a lot in common. He liked to camp and hike. *We could have been friends.*"

The story Colonel Moore told me was essentially the same one I would hear from other members of the Force. Understandably, the veterans were cautious when I approached them asking for information about "Lt. Mac." So many years after Ken's death, they still guarded the secret, unwilling to cause a fellow Forceman's loved ones any unnecessary pain. Once I assured them that I knew the truth, to a man they gave honest accounts.

Colonel Moore, like several others who weren't on the patrol, didn't know who shot Ken. The Colonel was sure, however, that the man must have been a replacement. He couldn't believe that a veteran Forceman could make such a mistake. The original members of the First Special Service Force were too well trained he told me; they had been lectured repeatedly to avoid making just such an error.

In the years after her visit to Ken's grave, Mother traveled frequently, her wanderlust undiminished by time. She lost none of her optimism over the years and never wavered in her belief that happiness is a choice.

My sisters and I moved often enough to allow her to combine family visits with new places to sightsee, and she thoroughly enjoyed herself. She went to Winston-Salem every year to spend a few weeks with her brothers and sisters, and usually made a short trip to Durham during her stay to see old friends from Duke and have tea with Angus. Mother didn't go back to 408 though. Mum had died in July of 1964, and Angus had moved to a smaller house only a few blocks from Swift Avenue. In 1978, dear, sweet Angus waltzed out of life much as he had waltzed through it, passing away as he slept at the age of 71.

Shortly after her eightieth birthday, Mother began to fail. My sisters and I first noticed a decline in her organizational skills, but that didn't alarm us. She had never been very organized. Eventually though, we couldn't mistake the fact that she could no longer care for herself. Her many health problems necessitated a level of care none of us felt capable of giving, so we moved her to a nursing home near me.

She kept some of her furnishings with her at the home, and that helped to minimize the institutional look of her room. The painting Angus had done for her so many years before, the one that had hung in our house, graced one wall. Her tabletops all but overflowed with pictures of her children and grandchildren, my father, and Ken. By her bedside she kept the collection of Dickens's works she had bought in England during the war, her photo albums, and every letter Ken had written her.

She gave me her beloved Treasure Chest when she moved, but it isn't quite so full anymore. Her most cherished possession – the wooden heart and chain that Ken carved during the long hours of night watch in Aspen – is gone, stolen in a burglary. The key that Ken carved to go with the necklace, the one he kept and wore around his neck, never made it to the box. It is in France, buried with him. The beautifully carved ivory necklace is gone too, a victim of the same thieves.

Jane still wears the cameo that Ken admired in some unnamed mountain village so very long ago. Before her health failed, Mother had given Jane the pin, fastened to the worn and faded blue cushion that had protected it on the long journey from Italy to North Carolina in 1944.

The ring Mother picked out to signify her engagement hasn't been in the box for years – Jane or I always wear it. The Easter card Ken stitched together at Anzio with its flat bouquet of flowers and leaves is still around, but it is framed now. The delicate flowers have not crumbled with age and are still discernable. Lily-of-the-Valley, perhaps.

There aren't many pictures of Ken left in the box. My sisters and I divided them among ourselves and each of us displays at least one in our home. We were somewhat surprised to discover that others find this a peculiar thing to do. To us it just seemed natural to group his picture with the rest of our family photographs.

Many missing items are unaccounted for. These are the things Jane, Anne, and I played with and lost over the years, before we had any idea how much they meant to our mother.

As Mother slowly lost touch with the world around her, she began to lose all memory of my father and their life together. She never forgot Ken though, and eventually his letters were the only clue I had that she was still connected. Once kept in neat bundles tied with blue ribbon, the letters lay scattered in a large box. Sometimes the box would be on her bed, sometimes in a chair or on the floor, but there was usually evidence that she had been sorting through it. By the last year or two of her life, Mother had lost the ability to read, but she still looked at Ken's letters, and touched them, as she held on to that last little bit of herself.

Mother had been a real beacon of light for my sisters and me, a sparkling North Star whose relentless optimism and strong moral compass guided us on our way. Inevitably though, she began to fail and she died the way stars do, collapsing into herself a bit more each day until there was little left of her. She grew frailer with each passing year, a victim of ill health and a series of small strokes. The strokes were the cruelest of her afflictions, eventually rendering my talkative mother mute.

In the years before she lost her ability to carry on a conversation, we talked about Ken many times. Still, I was more than a little surprised the day I dropped by for our afternoon visit and she greeted me with a huge smile and the news, "Kenneth came to see me last night!"

"Kenneth who?" I asked. She usually called him Ken, I didn't make the connection when she said Kenneth.

"You know, Kenneth!" she said emphatically. "He came to see me. I hadn't seen him in forever and we had such a wonderful visit. He stayed the longest time. It was so good to see him again."

Confused, and searching for some direction in our conversation, I asked her, "Are you talking about Ken? Do you mean Ken came to see you?"

She gave me a long, exasperated look and answered in a firm, quiet voice, "*Kenneth.*"

Kenneth Dougal McDougall

December 18, 1908 – September 15, 1944

Pearl Yarbrough Patterson

February 2, 1912 – March 30, 1999

Alton Dudley Patterson

July 19, 1904 – March 9, 1965

# Reflections on Reading a Sonnet by William Shakespeare

So long as men can breathe, or eyes can see
So long lives this, and this gived life to thee
Oh poet, who, in other days,
Wrote those immortal words of praise,
You little guessed, but I can see
You penned indeed a prophesy.
My breath is warm, my eyes are clear,
And I behold your lady dear.
More temperate than a summer's day,
She still outlives the mortal clay.
For Nature's course has not untrimmed,
Nor yet have Chance, nor ages dimmed
Those features that you loved so well
And strove in ringing words to tell.
I also love, I also hear
Death's winged chariot drawing near.
I too in song my love would save
From the chill fingers of the grave.
But Oh, alas! I lack your power
To lengthen out love's little hour.
Dead poet, teach me how to sing
Such happy songs that tears shall spring
To the bright eyes of other men!
That day will seem less bitter then
When Time and Death shall wrench apart
Her beauty, and my loving heart.

Kenneth McDougall

In Aspen, in the fall of 1942, Ken stole a few minutes of quiet time alone to read from a volume of Shakespeare. Sonnet XVIII, "Shall I compare thee to a summer's day?", inspired him to compose his own poem. He sent a copy to both Mum and Mother, the only correspondence he ever duplicated.

# Acknowledgments

This is the book my mother planned to write. No doubt it would have been a better book if she had been the author, but time ran out for her. Time ran out for almost everyone in this story long before I began my research. With very few exceptions, I have put this book together without the help of those whose story I am telling. Many times I have had to draw conclusions from conflicting information. I am sure that many of those conclusions were incorrect, but any mistakes were unintentional.

I have tried to remain true to Mother and Ken's story. This book was written so that Mother's descendants will know how bravely and honorably she lived her life. I can best illustrate that by telling the truth.

Although I sometimes combined the descriptions of similar activities to avoid redundancy, I have not embellished this beautiful story and have taken very little license with the events described. Most of my information came from Ken and Mother's wartime letters, and all quotes were taken directly from those letters, letters Ken wrote to Mum, or from conversations I personally witnessed. Mother's stories, combined with the letters, photographs, mementos, and paperwork that she left behind, provided an invaluable bridge to the life she led as a young woman.

Words could never express my gratitude to Angus for saving all of Ken's letters and papers, organizing them so beautifully, and then donating them to Duke University's archives. It has been my pleasure to locate the remaining McDougall descendants, and I remain grateful to them for letting Ken's voice speak so eloquently through this book.

Thomas Harkins and the staff at Duke's archives provided a great deal of help and I want to thank them as well as all the people in Durham who assisted me in my quest: Amelia Howle, Mary Pearse, Sally Feather, Betty Matthews, Grace Temple, Dot Wilkinson, and Dr. Ivan Brown who, at 93, shared with me in vivid detail what life had been like at a WWII army hospital in England. A special thanks to "the ladies at 408" for allowing me to revisit my childhood.

I want to thank Debbie Gemar, the 10th Mountain Division's incredibly patient former archivist/librarian for her hard work on my behalf. I would never have gotten this story off the ground without her considerable help. I am grateful to Ralph Lafferty, Ken's lieutenant at Aspen, for filling in details about Ken's time there, and to the many men of the 10th Mountain Division who tried so hard to help me in my search.

I am indebted to the men of the First Special Service Force who told me the truth about Ken's death, beginning with Bob Moore and including those on that fateful patrol: Cy Mermelstein, Ed Wolfe, Clarence Bean, Maurice White, and Harry Weaver. I want to thank the above mentioned men, as well as Jordan Markson, Noe Salinas, and Ed Thomas, for sharing with me such kind memories of Ken. And my warmest remembrances to the Forcemen who went back up the mountain and brought Ken's body down: Cy Mermelstein, Ed Wolfe, Harry Weaver and Ernie Brown.

Thank you also to Gordon Sims and Bill Story for sharing the history of the FSSF with me, enabling me to better interpret Ken's letters. In my research, I relied heavily on Robert Burhans's book, The First Special Service Force, as well as Robert Todd Ross's book, The Supercommandos, and I am grateful to both authors for their historically accurate accounts.

I also want to express gratitude to Roderick De Normann for his research. In the years since WWII, some of the details concerning the POW escape attempt from Camp 23 have not held up under scrutiny. De Normann's book, For Führer and Fatherland, thoroughly examines both the actual events of the "Devizes Plot" and the mindset of those involved. While I tried to keep further distortion of the story to a minimum, it would have been unfair to Mother not to present the situation as closely as possible to the way she actually lived it. She never had the benefit of hindsight, and the events as she understood them were a defining experience for her.

The men who fought in WWII have tried hard to forget the horrible things they saw. More than sixty years after the war, the memories that come back tend to filter through in bits and pieces. I have tried to weave together those divergent strands and no doubt I have failed at times. Please know that my intentions were honorable.

Thank you to Diana and Colin Hallward for the many kindnesses they showed a stranger in Devizes. A special thanks to Diana for answering my endless questions over the years and making such an effort to help me gather the information I needed.

I want to thank my husband John for the long hours he spent making a stack of old, creased photos look worthy of their place in this book, and for his loving support during the four years that this project overshadowed our life.

Thanks too, to Jo Barksdale, Karen Dieckmann, and Jane Boykin for their help editing this book, and Anne Patterson for sharing her memories. It is a far better book because of their help.

A special thanks to my friends and family who encouraged me and urged me to write this story – thank you for believing I could do this. I wasn't nearly so sure.

And last, I want to thank my parents – my mother for not letting this beautiful story die with Ken, and my father, whose generosity allowed me to know that there was a story to tell.

# About the Author

Susan Lentz resides in Nashville, Tennessee, with her husband and two sons. She is currently collaborating on a book about the legendary First Special Service Force, America's first Special Forces unit.

Printed in the United States
82311LV00001B/181-288